Building A Firm Foundation

A Pre-Marital Counseling Guide

Rev. Richard W. Gilbert

WESTBOW
PRESS®
A DIVISION OF THOMAS NELSON
& ZONDERVAN

WestBow Press books may be ordered through booksellers or by contacting:

WestBow Press
A Division of Thomas Nelson & Zondervan
1663 Liberty Drive
Bloomington, IN 47403
www.westbowpress.com
844-714-3454

ISBN: 978-1-6642-4171-8 (sc)
ISBN: 978-1-6642-4170-1 (e)

Print information available on the last page.

WestBow Press rev. date: 8/20/2021

Acknowledgments

The telephone rings, and the voice on the other end says, "my fiancé and I are planning to get married, and we were wondering if you would be able to perform the ceremony for us." Sometimes the couple is part of our church and many times they are not. With each of these is the responsibility of not only helping them for the events of the "Big Day" but of preparing them for a lifetime together.

I am greatly indebted to all the young couples that God has privileged me to work with over these years at Niagara Frontier Bible Church. They have challenged me to think through very carefully what I have said in their pre-marital counseling. Their eager participation has greatly encouraged me as we have worked together. Their constructive comments have helped to continually refine these materials.

I am extremely grateful to Mary Bugay, my very competent and ever-faithful administrative assistant. In the midst of pressing needs from numerous directions, she has brought this book to print.

Most of all, I am indebted to my wife, Lynette. She is a woman of God who has taught me the meaning of love; daily demonstrating it in her life. I am so thankful that God has allowed us to share our lives together.

Contents

Introduction

The family in our twenty-first century western culture is under attack; an attack that does not appear to be letting up. Current statistics indicate that approximately fifty-five percent of secular marriages are ending in divorce. While these figures are somewhat shocking, even more alarming is the realization that the success-failure rate for Christian marriages is <u>not</u> much different.

God has given the pastor the responsibility of the spiritual welfare of his congregation. Pre-marital counseling is one way to deal with the problem of the disintegration of marriage. Just as we do preventative maintenance on our automobiles to keep them in smooth running condition, we need to do preventative maintenance for marriages. With the high failure rate of marriages and the number of stresses that appear to be working overtime to fracture the marriage relationship, it only makes good sense to put forth <u>every</u> effort to insure the success of the new marriage.

The couple has already invested considerable time and money in their relationship. Why increase their failure potential, when an additional small time investment will geometrically increase their marriage success potential? Why plan to fail, when a consistent and carefully followed approach will help insure the success of the most important adventure upon which a man and woman will ever embark? Pre-marital counseling is a way of addressing and working through problems before they come to the surface. Various strengths and weaknesses in the couple's interaction can be examined within the counseling context. Suggestions can be then made to assist them in working through potential problem situations to a satisfactory resolution.

Regardless of how well they think they know one another, the couple anticipating marriage has many issues they have not even begun to discuss. Some of these are seen to be of no consequence, some of assumed agreement, and some so emotionally laden that they are avoided at all costs. One of the primary purposes of any pre-marital counseling program is to generate discussion in some of these "overlooked" areas.

As we begin this pre-marital counseling course there are many things that we wish to accomplish and a number of issues that we will discuss together. While this course is not designed to be an extensive examination of all scriptures covering the marital relationship, at the same time the biblical foundation for marriage and the individual roles of the husband and wife will be presented. Throughout this book the Word of God will be brought to bear upon the particular issue being discussed.

Basically, the material presented will address the situations and problems that arise in day-to-day marital living. Unfortunately, limited time and space does not permit as detailed an analysis of the issues as we would like.

Having worked with many couples over these past years and seeing the time constraints that are upon them, I have sought to keep the required number of sessions to a minimum. At the same time, there is a wealth of information that must be addressed if we are to prepare the couple to succeed in this lifelong blessing from God.

Some of the material is presented in workbook format, requiring the couple to individually record their responses and then discuss those answers with their partner. In this way communication is promoted, and the issues are carefully and fairly addressed by each person. All Scripture quotations presented are taken from the New International Version of the Bible.

In addition to this manual, couples are encouraged to work with a minister or counselor who uses one of the many excellent personal assessment tools that are currently available. I have used Prepare/Enrich[1] since 1989 and have been very satisfied with the results. This requires one session (forty-five minutes) to administer the assessment tool and two follow-up discussion sessions (one hour each).

The way that the material in this pre-marital counseling manual is handled will vary with the minister or counselor with whom you are working. If you are using this yourself, without assistance, you will want to work through the sessions one at a time. If you are a minister or counselor using this material with a couple planning to marry, you will probably need to combine some of the chapters, to limit the actual number of sessions that you meet with them. Appendix C gives a suggested counseling schedule, combining the Prepare/Enrich assessment text and the material in this manual.

1

Biblical Foundation
For Marriage

Rev. Richard W. Gilbert

Marriage is a commitment that a couple makes to one another, a commitment that is to last the rest of their lives. It is not something that is to be entered capriciously, nor is it something to which the participants bring less than their full effort. Regardless of the events of daily life, the presence or absence of the feeling of love, or the changes in one another, this commitment is to be present. Commitment to one another is an act of the will. Each of you must choose to be committed to your partner. With that commitment present, you can now begin to work on making your marriage all that God wants it to be.

If your marriage is going to have a good start, you must understand what the Word of God has to say about this new relationship. There are many places to begin examining Scriptural admonitions, but the one to which we will address our attention is Genesis 2:18-25,

> "The Lord God said, 'it is not good for the man to be alone. I will make a helper suitable for him.' Now the Lord God had formed out of the ground all the beasts of the field and all the birds of the air. He brought them to the man to see what he would name them; and whatever the man called each living creature, that was its name. So the man gave names to all the livestock, the birds of the air and all the beasts of the field. But for Adam no suitable helper was found. So the Lord God caused the man to fall into a deep sleep; and while he was sleeping, he took one of the man's ribs and closed up the place with flesh. Then the Lord God made a woman from the rib he had taken out of the man and he brought her to the man. The man said, "This is now bone of my bones and flesh of my flesh; she shall be called woman, for she was taken out of man." For this reason a man will leave his father and mother and be united to his wife, and they will become one flesh. The man and his wife were both naked, and they felt no shame."

There are many principles that we can draw from this passage. First, the idea of male and female was God's idea. The propagation of the species was not something that amazingly developed over millions of years of evolution. God made the man and woman just as they are, in fulfillment of his divine plan for the race. The sovereign wisdom of God conceived the wonderful mysteries of male and female, masculinity and femininity, to bring joy into our lives.

Second, marriage was designed by God to meet the first problem of the human race: loneliness. God had made the earth and everything upon it. He made all the animals and placed Adam there to have dominion over them. But, "for Adam no suitable helper was found" (Genesis 2:20b). Adam was lonely! Within reach were any number of creatures that Adam could pet and talk to, but there were none with whom he could actually communicate. In a crowded garden the man was alone; something which God had said "was not good" (Genesis 2:18a). So, a wise and loving Creator-Father provided a perfect solution for Adam. He made another creature just like him, and yet so wonderfully different from him. God made a "helper suitable for him" (Genesis 2:18b). The loneliness that Adam had experienced was now replaced by a vibrant, dynamic relationship with another person who would meet the needs in his life; just as he would meet the needs in her life.

Third, marriage was planned and decreed to bring happiness, not misery to mankind. God's evaluation of all of His creation was that "it was very good" (Genesis 1:31). Adam now had both communication and companionship. He now had someone with whom to share his thoughts, his life, his dreams, his heart. This new relationship brought happiness.

Fourth, God directs husbands and wives to leave their fathers and mothers. Marriage must begin with a leaving of all other relationships in order to establish a permanent relationship between one man and one woman. The bonds of love with one's parents are lasting ones, but these ties are now changed in character so that the man's full commitment is now to his wife. Accordingly, the wife's full commitment is now to her husband. "Leaving" does not necessarily mean that a physical move out of the area is required. It does mean, however, that the couple's relationship to their parents should now be much different than it was in the past. They are establishing a home of their own, and no longer is their relationship with their parents the primary one.

Fifth, they are to cleave to one another. Marriage requires an inseparable joining of husband and wife throughout their lifetime. They are to be "glued" together; nothing being able to separate them. Several years ago a new glue product, Superglue, came upon the market. This new glue was so permanent that once the two surfaces were adhered together, nothing would be able to separate them. This is the level of commitment that God expects to be in the marriage relationship, nothing able to separate them!

In today's society the destruction of a marriage is as easy as changing one's clothing. Divorces in almost all states have "no fault" clauses and in some places can be obtained in as little as three weeks. What a far cry that is from God's command to cleave to one another, not to separate that which God has joined (Mark 10:9).

Finally, they are to be one flesh. This refers primarily to the sexual relationship in marriage. The sexual union is a natural and necessary part of marriage. But, becoming one flesh involves much more than just the physical union. It is an intimacy of hearts, minds, emotions, spirits and bodies. As one marriage counselor has described it, "marriage is the total commitment of the total person for the total life."[2] This is the extent of the one-flesh relationship that God says is to be present in your marriage.

This is the marriage design ordained by God Himself at the beginning of man's history on this earth. This bonding relationship between the man and woman is deep, tender, pure, intimate, patterned after Christ's love for His bride: the Church. This is the foundation for the love-life that God wants you to have in your marriage. "And God saw all that He had made, and it was very good!

QUESTIONS FOR PERSONAL REFLECTION AND COUPLE INTERACTION

1. One of the purposes of marriage was to solve the problem of man's loneliness. Paraphrase Genesis 2:18-24 to show how God met that need.

2. What are some of the results of companionship mentioned in Genesis 2:24?

3. When did God institute marriage? What does that say to you about how God views marriage? How are we to view marriage?

4. Why do you want to get married? What will marriage provide for you that you do not already have?

5. Why do you want to marry your fiancé? Please give reasons; include those qualities that caused you to choose him/her.

6. What qualities are you bringing to this relationship to make it work? Please list at least six.

7. What does the term "leave father and mother" mean to you? How will this be accomplished in your marriage?

2

Spiritual Growth In Marriage

Marriage counselors and marriage manuals, both secular and Christian, are filled with instructions on things that you can do to build a successful marriage. While there is no disagreement with the principles presented, in order for them to work they must be built upon a solid foundation. If a man is going to fulfill the spiritual role of husband, he must first <u>be</u> a spiritual man. If a wife is going to fulfill the spiritual role of wife, she must first <u>be</u> a spiritual woman. To that end, it is necessary to consider what kind of a person you <u>are</u> before you can concern yourself with what you should <u>do</u>.

Have you ever looked closely at a braided rope? It is usually composed of three separate strands that are woven together. A rope of three strands has tremendous tensile strength, but it is only as strong as its individual strands. The same thing is true about the marriage relationship. It is only as strong as the individual members of that relationship. A Christian marriage has three separate components, as the three-strand braided rope. Those three components are the husband, the wife, and God. God certainly is the strongest of the three strands and never fails in his role. It is the other two strands, the husband or the wife, that are sometimes weak. When one of them is weak, then the marriage itself is weak.

In his letter to the church at Ephesus, the Apostle Paul gave clear instructions for how the husband and wife were to conduct themselves within the home.[3] It is here, focusing upon the biblical roles of the individual marriage partners, that the primary emphasis is usually placed. To do that, however, is to miss the most important part of Paul's instruction. Before telling husbands and wives what they should <u>do</u>, Paul was very careful to tell them what they should <u>be</u>.[4] Notice his instructions to the Ephesian believers, and to us, in Ephesians 5:1, 2, 18:

> "Be imitators of God, therefore, as dearly loved children and live a life of love, just as Christ loved us and gave himself up for us as a fragrant offering and sacrifice to God...Do not get drunk on wine, which leads to debauchery. Instead, be filled with the Spirit."

If you are going to fulfill the spiritual roles of husband and wife, you must first be a man and woman of God. You need to have a living, dynamic relationship with the Lord Jesus Christ. It is not something that one partner can do for the other. Each person needs to be growing in their individual personal relationship with the Lord.

The Word of God gives very clear mandates for everyone to study God's Word and pray:

> "Like newborn babies, crave pure spiritual milk, so that you may grow up in your salvation" (1 Peter 2:2).

> "Do your best to present yourself to God as one approved, a workman who does not need to be ashamed and who correctly handles the word of truth" (2 Timothy 2:15).

> "And pray in the Spirit on all occasions with all kinds of prayers and requests. With this in mind, be alert and always keep on praying for all the saints" (Ephesians 6:18).

In addition to your individual growth in Jesus Christ, as a couple you need to fellowship in a local church. The importance of this corporate interaction cannot be underestimated, as noted in Hebrews 10:24-25:

> "And let us consider how we may spur one another on toward love and good deeds. Let us not give up meeting together, as some are in the habit of doing, but let us encourage one another- and all the more as you see the Day approaching.

Rev. Richard W. Gilbert

As you individually build your lives and together build your home upon the clear principles of the Word of God, bathing everything in prayer, there is nothing that will ever be able to sever the marriage that God is establishing.

QUESTIONS FOR PERSONAL REFLECTION AND COUPLE INTERACTION

1. Are you sure that you are a child of God? How do you know that you have been forgiven of your sins?

2. Are you <u>now</u> having an individual (personal) time with God? What are you doing to develop in your spiritual walk?

3. Do you and your fiancé spend time together reading God's Word and praying? What are your plans for this after you are married? How will it be accomplished?

4. Do you now attend a church? To what extent are you active in that church?

5. After your marriage where will you attend church? How will you serve the Lord individually and as a couple in that church?

6. How will you teach your children about Jesus Christ?

3

Biblical Roles In Marriage

Social scientists and psychological theorists have a myriad of ideas for how marriage "should" work, yet there is only one set of instructions that explain how it will "best" work. For a marriage to function properly we need to look at the instructions that have been written by the One who designed and implemented marriage itself. God's instruction for marriage is found in His Word: the Bible.

The most comprehensive presentation of biblical roles is found in Ephesians 5:22-33, and it is to that passage that your attention is now directed. Each of the two roles will be examined separately, with that of the husband being presented first.

The Husband's Role

While the wife's role is presented first in text, it is the husband whom God holds responsible for the spiritual leadership of the home. While each person is accountable for their own individual response to the Holy Spirit's leading, the husband is accountable for himself <u>and</u> the spiritual development of all those within his home. Ephesians 5:25-30 presents the husband's role:

> "Husbands, love your wives just as Christ loved, the church and gave himself up for her to make her holy, cleansing her by the washing with water through the word, and to present her to himself as a radiant church, without stain or wrinkle or any other blemish, but holy and blameless. In this way, husbands ought to love their wives as their own bodies. He who loves his wife loves himself. After all, no one ever hated his own body, but he feeds and cares for it, just as Christ does the church--for we are members of his body."

It is amazing the way that people selectively read God's Word.

Many husbands see the words, "for the husband is the head of the wife" (v.23) but fail to see that it is grounded in the level of love that Christ had for the church. They fail to see that they will not be able to lead their homes the way that God indicates if they don't love their wives the way that God commands.

When the apostle Paul states that husbands are to love as Christ loved the church, what kind of a love is he speaking about? Jesus said "I am the good shepherd, the good shepherd gives his life for the sheep" (John 10:11). Jesus was more concerned about the sheep (mankind) than he was for his own personal safety. His love was an unselfish, sacrificial love. Jesus' own description of this love will help you to see its true nature; "greater love has no one than this, that he lay down his life for his friends" (John 15:13). Jesus' concern for himself was secondary to his concern for the human race.

A husband expressing this level of love is willing to give all that his wife requires; willing to make any sacrifice that will bring good to her. He is willing to give up anything and everything for her; even his very life.

The apostle Peter gives some additional insight into the quality of love that the husband is to have for his wife.

> "Husbands, in the same way be considerate as you
> live with your wives, and treat them with respect
> as the weaker partner and heirs with you of the
> gracious gift of life..." (1 Peter 3:7).

Peter is not saying that women are inferior to men, but on the contrary he states that they are "joint-heirs" of eternal life. Both husbands and wives are recipients of the gracious gift of life from God!

The phrase "weaker partner" might be better understood by the term "delicate vase," for that is the imagery that Peter is presenting. The woman is like a delicate vase that needs to be handled with loving care. Peter is looking at the attitude that is to be behind the love demonstrated. The wife is to be treated with special tender loving care by her husband.

The Wife's Role

The wife's role in the marriage is presented in Ephesians 5:22-24:

> "Wives, submit to your husbands as to the Lord. For the husband is the head of the wife as Christ is the head of the church, his body, of which he is the Savior. Now as the church submits to Christ, so also wives should submit to their husbands in everything."

While Genesis 2 indicates that the wife is a companion and helper to her husband, Paul focuses upon a different aspect of their relationship. He focuses attention upon the attitude that is behind their interaction; indicating that the foundational attitude of the wife is to be one of submission.

When God judged Adam and Eve for their sin in the Garden of Eden, part of the judgment on Eve was that Adam "will rule over you" (Genesis 3:16b). That was the beginning of the struggle, for no one wants to constantly submit to another person. That struggle has continued in intensity with each generation; primarily because of a failure to understand what submission really means.

The word submit is the Greek word "hupotasso," which means "to put in a place or position under someone or something." It is a military term meaning to rank in terms of function not equality. There are many things that submission does <u>not</u> mean to a wife. It does not mean that the wife is inferior to her husband. It does not mean that she never opens her mouth and gives an opinion. It does not mean that she is a slave or a "doormat" to be walked upon by her husband. It does not mean that she sits quietly on the sidelines and never uses the talents that she possesses. It does not mean that she is like a pawn on a chessboard; to be moved about as her husband desires.

Submission for the woman is not a negative concept but a positive one. Submission is mandated by God because it will bring good, not bad, into the relationship. Submission means that the wife is under the direction and leadership of her husband. In the marriage relationship one person is ultimately held responsible, and that person is the husband. Submission is planning, preparing, praying and deciding together. Sometimes, however, there will not be a unified decision. An issue may have been discussed at length, and still the husband and wife disagree on the course of action. At that time God tells the wife to defer to the one whom He holds responsible: the husband.

Our society has instituted a system of traffic laws to help control the flow of vehicles upon the highways. These laws are not conditional; stating that each driver will obey only when the other drivers obey. The laws state "matter of factly" that each driver will obey. Obeying the traffic laws is in the best interest of each motorist on the road; helping him to safely reach his destination.

The biblical roles for each marriage partner are similar to the traffic laws. They are there to help each person reach their destination: a growing, vibrant, loving relationship with one another. As with traffic laws, the biblical marital roles are unconditional. Each marriage partner is to do his part! When each one does his part, then the destination of a life-long marriage is reached together.

Throughout this chapter the assumption has been made that each of the marriage partners knows what love is. That assumption may be valid or erroneous. While most people use the word "love" very freely, and at times carelessly, they have little understanding of all that it entails. In chapter six we will look in detail at the meaning of the word "love;" especially within the context of marriage.

QUESTIONS FOR PERSONAL REFLECTION
AND COUPLE INTERACTION

1. Someone has said that Paul was only reflecting society's view of marriage and that these principles are not binding in every age. Do you agree or disagree? Why?

2. Husbands are to love their wives as Christ loved the church. What does that mean to you?

3. What should a wife expect of a husband who is being obedient to the biblical role as stated by Paul?

4. Please list six ways that you can demonstrate sacrificial love to your wife.

5. Define "submission" (check a dictionary). List four implications of submission for a wife.

6. Is it possible for a woman to disagree with her husband and still be in submission to him? How?

7. How can you demonstrate this level of commitment in your relationship with your husband?

8. In light of Ephesians 5:21, is submission only for the wife? Give three examples where the husband could submit to the wife.

9. What do you feel the consequences will be if one or the other marriage partners fails to follow these instructions? Be specific.

10. How will you respond if your fiancé does not fulfill the Biblical role he/she is to have in marriage?

11. What will you do if there is an impasse in a discussion with your fiancé and a decision must be made?

4

Purposes Of Engagement

One Chicago social scientist has said that the way a couple handles the invitation list, flower arrangements, and inevitable tensions and hassles of their wedding day is a good test of how well their marriage will work.

Unfortunately, couples who fail this test and begin to suspect that they may not be meant for each other generally are not likely to call off the wedding. They proceed ahead as if nothing was wrong. The engagement period is rarely used by the couple to prepare for married life, in terms of resolving some of the problems that they are likely to face. Instead, most of their efforts during that time are focused upon the hundreds of details that must be worked out for the wedding ceremony.

For a successful wedding ceremony and reception, there are many decisions that the couple must make. Their ideas, desires and personal tastes must be integrated with those of their parents and peers; all within the parameters of the amount of money available for the "big day." Some couples see this as a great opportunity to work together, while others place these responsibilities and details primarily into the hands of the prospective bride. One young groom said, "I don't care what they plan and do; just as long as I get the girl in the end!"

Regardless of how the final details are determined, planning the wedding can be a time of growth in the couple's relationship as each learns how to "give and take;" negotiating a mutually satisfying result.

The engagement period is much more than merely the days and weeks following the giving of the engagement ring. It is more than the few months needed for planning the ceremony. It is a time during which the couple draws closer and closer to one another. It is a time during which their knowledge and understanding of one another deepens. It is a time during which the thousands of previous conversations now become more specific and directed toward certain goals.

In the space below please list what you believe to be at least five purposes for the engagement period.

1.
2.
3.
4.
5.

Howard and Charlotte Clinebell, <u>The Intimate Marriage</u>, state that there are three periods in any marital relationship known as "crises of intimacy." These are the engagement period, the early years following the honeymoon, and the time when the children leave the home to establish their own lives. During the first crisis period, the engagement period, they indicate that there are a number of goals that are pursued.[5]

The following are some of the purposes of the engagement period, adapted from the above authors, with additional insights added. This list is not intended to be exhaustive but to help you begin to see how important this period of time is in your lives together as a couple.

First, the engagement period is a time in which the couple is learning to think in terms of a family unit rather than as individuals. They begin to learn to consider their partner's needs over and above their own (Philippians 2:3-4).

Second, it is a time of reconditioning unwholesome attitudes toward the opposite sex. Through dating experiences and stereotypes the couple has generally developed some wrong attitudes about the opposite sex. Many of their personal views have been formulated from the input of peers rather than biblical principles and sociological or psychological standards of behavior. During the engagement period the couple learns some of the many male-female differences and similarities that are present. While they may have thought that they previously knew the opposite sex, this is now a time of greater awareness and understanding.

Third, the engagement period is a time to consider family backgrounds, past experiences and how they affect the new relationship, especially in the area of expectations. The Clinebells state,

> "conflict of role expectancies...is the clash between the inner images or pictures which each partner brings to the marriage, of what constitutes "right" roles for men-women, husbands - wives, fathers-mothers. Every person brings literally dozens of these images, absorbed unconsciously in his family-of-origin. These inner pictures tend to determine how he feels and behaves and how he expects his mate to feel and behave in the varied roles each takes in marriage".[6]

Because of the different and numerous expectations that are carried from single life into the marital union, these often generate personal frustration and result in conflict in the couple's relationship. It is during the engagement period that these differing and often contrasting expectations need to be discussed and resolved.

Fourth, the engagement period is a time to develop goals both as individuals and as a couple. It is a time to talk together of mutual interests, dreams, and the steps that can be taken to accomplish them. The couple then can begin to take deliberate steps to reach those joint goals.

Fifth, the engagement period is a time to continue individual growth and development. When two people marry, they do not lose their individual distinctiveness, but instead maintain that distinctiveness; bringing it into the marriage to enrich every part of the relationship.

A favorite song at Christmas time is "Frosty the Snowman."

"Frosty" was more than just a lot of snow rolled up into three different sized balls. In addition to the snow, he had a silk hat, a corn cob pipe, a button for a nose, two pieces of coal for eyes, and a scarf around his neck. All of these items maintained their own individuality, yet at the same time all of them together made up the person of "Frosty". That is the same thing that happens in marriage. Two different individual people enter into a new composite relationship: marriage. They form a bond; they are now a couple, a new family. Yet in the midst of that family they still maintain their individual uniqueness and distinctiveness. The engagement period is a time to focus on both your individual growth, your special uniqueness, and it is a time to focus on your joint life together.

Sixth, the engagement period is a time to discuss attitudes and plans for work and family finances. Many couples tend to underestimate the stress level upon marriages from lack of money or poor money management. Several surveys have reported that many of the marriages that break up in the first two years do so because of money disagreements. This is a time to find out how your partner handles money. It is a time to mutually decide upon what type of lifestyle you want to live. Among the many things that need to be considered and discussed are work position, educational level, previous lifestyle, and personal debt load. This issue will be further discussed in chapter ten.

Seventh, this is a time to begin exploring attitudes toward children and discipline. When will you have children? How many children do you want to have? What kind of discipline will be used in your home? The key here is unity. This issue will be further discussed in chapter sixteen.

Eighth, it is a time to continue perfecting your communication skills. Nothing is as easy as talking, and yet one of the most difficult things that we can do is to communicate. At the same time, communications is absolutely vital in the marital relationship. Part of the root cause of almost every interpersonal struggle in marriage is the lack of communication. There may be a number of different precipitating causes, but generally the root problem is a failure to communicate about the central issue under consideration. Chapter seven will present additional insight on this issue.

Ninth, the engagement period is a time to begin the development of an intimate relationship. This is to include every area of interpersonal relationship, <u>except</u> the sexual area. That level of intimacy must wait for its development until the marriage begins. Further discussion on premarital sex is found in chapter five and a discussion of sex in marriage in chapter fifteen.

Finally, the engagement period is a time for planning the general and specific details of the wedding. Chapter thirteen of this manual provides more information on this subject.

As you can easily see, the engagement period is a crucial time in the life of the couple as they continue on their path toward marriage. It is a time in which much is done and much is discussed as they seek to determine whether this is the union that God would have for them for life.

There are some danger signals that may come into view during the engagement period which should cause the couple to delay their wedding plans until they have straightened out those problem areas. These problem areas are like icebergs; only a portion of them may be visible at the present time, but they will come totally to the surface in the relationship after the marriage ceremony. Some of these danger signals follow.

A general uneasy feeling about the relationship; a lack of inner peace is a danger signal. This is a nagging, aching, disturbing feeling "inside" that says "something's wrong".

Frequent arguments are a danger signal. You are never sure how the date will end. There seems to be more fighting present than fun.

Avoiding the discussion of sensitive subjects is a danger signal. You're afraid of hurting your partner's feelings or of starting an argument. You find yourself thinking, "I'd better not talk about this."

Getting more involved physically is a danger signal. You resolve to limit the acceleration of your physical intimacy, but find that on each new date you start again at the place where you left off. Sometimes couples get involved physically as a way to avoid arguments.

You find yourself always doing what your partner wants to do. You are constantly giving in, being accommodating. It may be that your partner is very domineering or that you are very insecure, or a combination of both.

Detection of serious emotional disturbances such as extreme fears, extreme shyness, bizarre behavior, irrational anger, inflicting physical injury, inability to demonstrate affection are all danger signals.

If you feel you are staying in the relationship because of fear, this is a danger signal.

Apparent or real hypochondria by your future partner is a danger area. They are constantly complaining about aches and pains and going from doctor to doctor.

Poor personal motivation and money management is a danger area. Your partner continually makes excuses for not finding a job, or frequently borrows money from you. The partner who evades responsibility and who can't manage his money wisely will be a poor marriage risk.

A partner who is overly jealous, suspicious, questioning your word all the time is a danger area. Additionally, if your partner is a perfectionist or constantly critical, it should raise a "red flag" before you. If he or she cannot accept constructive criticism or does not apologize when wrong, you should have serious concerns about the relationship.

How does your partner treat you? If he or she treats you contemptuously or with sarcasm, this should immediately signal a danger area.

If parents and other significant people in your life are opposed to your marriage, this should signal a danger area. You should consider their reasons before you make a final decision.

If you have <u>few</u> areas of common interest, you need to step back and look again at your relationship. While part of the excitement of marriage is introducing one's partner to new ideas and activities, there needs to be <u>some</u> common ground upon which to start.

Last, but certainly not least, if there is no spiritual harmony between the two of you, the danger flag should immediately begin to wave! If your intended spouse is not a Christian, you need to immediately terminate <u>all</u> marriage plans. God has said that a believer and a non-believer are <u>not</u> to be joined together.[7] When that principle is violated, all that results is grief in the relationship. Additionally, if there is a great difference in the level of spiritual growth between the two people in the relationship, a danger signal should come up as well. This is not saying that the marriage will not work, but it indicates that it will bring with it some additional problems as well.

The engagement period is not a time that can be taken lightly. Instead much effort must be expended by both parties in the relationship, and as this is happening, great rewards will result!

<u>QUESTIONS FOR PERSONAL REFLECTION AND COUPLE INTERACTION</u>

1. To the prospective bride: what do you expect from your husband?

2. To the prospective groom: what do you expect from your wife?

3. What do you think your fiancé expects from you?

4. To what extent are these expectations reasonable? Why?

5. To what extent are they unreasonable? Why?

6. What will you do if your fiancé does not live up to your expectations?

7. What steps are you going to take for individual growth during the engagement period?

8. What steps are you going to take to help strengthen your bond as a couple?

9. What are two goals you have as a couple for year 1? Year 5? Year 10?

5

Physical Relationship During Engagement Period

Rev. Richard W. Gilbert

As we consider the societies of ages past, one of the things that clearly comes to the forefront is the decadence, the sexual immorality that permeated many of them. The last two world empires, Greece and Rome, of which much information exists, were saturated and at times obsessed with sex.

Taking a long, careful, analytical look at our twenty-first century Western culture, we see amazing similarities to what has gone before. Our society places an enormous emphasis upon sex. We see it on television, in the newspapers, advertising media, etc. Everywhere we turn we are told that sex is the answer to whatever our need is. A myriad of products are sold using sexual allurement as the motivation for their purchase. From shaving cream to automobiles, from pizza to frying pans, sex is the allurement that advertisers use to market their product. If we believe all that we are seeing in the media, it is not love that makes the world go around, but sex!

We do not live in a Christian nation, but our country was founded upon Christian principles. Since those beginning years, however, our nation has stepped further and further away from those principles. In the past thirty years we have sunk further into the morass of immorality. Thirty years ago, in this country, a person who <u>was</u> sexually active before or outside of marriage was not the norm and was generally looked down upon. That has all changed, for now the person who is <u>not</u> sexually active before marriage is considered to be abnormal. Normal acceptable behavior in our society today is sexual activity totally apart from any marriage relationship. The person who believes in sexual abstinence outside of marriage is seen to be behind the times and a little bit "weird." Attempting to hold the abstinence position often brings the person contempt and scorn from contemporaries.

But, if the sexual revolution is so great, if the freedom to be sexually active is wonderful and right, then what about all of the results from that freedom? What about the 204,000 people who have already died from AIDS in the United States?[8] Even if half were from

IV drug usage and secondary infection, that still leaves over 100,000 people afflicted through sexual activity.

If being sexually active apart from marriage is so right, then what about the one million plus unmarried teenage girls that give birth to children every year; girls who are then locked into a future of poverty and hopelessness.

If being sexually active apart from marriage is so right, then why are over one and one-half million babies aborted in the United States every year? Why are these lives destroyed to pay the price for the sexual activity of their parents?

If being sexually active apart from marriage is so right, then why has the divorce rate steadily increased each year? One would think that the more couples were intimately involved before marriage, the greater would be their chances of a stable life-long relationship. The data, however, does not support such assumptions.

Our sex-saturated society has blurred and distorted the beauty and joy of growing into the sexual relationship of marriage as described in Scripture. The biblical guidelines for the physical act of marriage is found in Genesis 2:24; "they shall become one flesh." Then, in Genesis 4:1 it says "Adam lay with his wife Eve, and she became pregnant and gave birth to Cain." The Hebrew text literally says that Adam "knew" his wife. The sexual relationship is much more than just the physical act of intercourse but instead grows out of the intimacy that the couple shares at every level in their relationship.

As in the other levels of communication and intimacy within the marriage, in the sexual area the couple will learn together, grow together, struggle together, and continue to learn throughout their lifetime. The beginning of this learning process is during the engagement period.

In chapter four we discussed the fact that the engagement period was a time in which the development of an intimate relationship continues on every level except for the sexual level. Yet, during the engagement period there will also be physical intimacy present.

The question is "what parameters or limits are to be set for that intimacy?" How far should a couple go in their intimacy?

Before that question is answered, there is another question that needs to first be addressed. That is the question which every Christian couple must answer: "why should we wait?" Many think that because they are committed to one another then it is all right to take the final step and have total sexual intimacy. After all they are engaged and will soon be married. A number of recent studies have shown that as many as fifty percent of people getting married have previously been engaged. An engagement ring does not guarantee that you will marry that person.

If we look at the world's rationale and value structure, there is no reason for waiting. Consequently, most people in the world today do not wait until marriage to have sexual intercourse. They are sexually active at younger and younger ages, with first time sexual intercourse often at the 11-12 year old level.

As we come to Scripture, we see the sanctity in which God holds the physical relationship in marriage. "Marriage should be honored by all, and the marriage bed kept pure, for God will judge the adulterer and all the sexually immoral" (Hebrews 13:4). God's Word, from the Ten Commandments to Christ's teachings, upholds the sanctity of the sexual relationship in marriage and condemns its practice outside of marriage. Those involved in sexual intercourse outside of their own marriage are breaking God's standard, and He will judge them. They are taking that which God said was "very good"[9] and perverting it to their own selfish use. They are taking that which God has said is holy, clean, pure and righteous and turning it into sin!

The world says, "I love you, and I want to make love with you." Based upon its empty value structure, it believes these feelings and desires are enough to justify sharing this final level of intimacy with one another. According to God's standard, however, this is not nearly enough! God says that there is to be also a criteria of commitment to one another. They are to "leave" and "cleave" to one another and then through that to share in the intimacy of the one-flesh relationship.

Given the conviction to refrain from sexual intercourse until marriage, the previous question may now be addressed. "How far can a couple go in physical intimacy before marriage?" There is a general principle that applies here: that which has its natural end in sexual intercourse should be reserved to the wedding night and thereafter.

This means that you should not engage in any physical activity, such as heavy petting, that will build up the other person's sexual drives to the point of no return. Participating at this level of involvement only brings frustration from your physical relationship, rather than the joy that God wants to be there. The apostle Peter warns us of the devil's subtleties and viciousness.[10] One area in which he consistently attacks with devastating accuracy and success is that of the pre-marital physical relationship. As a general principle of Christian interpersonal relationships, we are to do nothing which causes our brother (or sister) to stumble.[11] Thus, both you and your partner must be sensitive to one another and place the other's spiritual health ahead of your personal desire for physical fulfillment at the present moment. As a couple you need to make Jesus Christ the Lord of every area of your life, including your sexual life. You need to wait for the green light from Him, and that comes at your wedding.

There are several benefits that come from waiting until marriage for complete sexual intimacy. Some of these are as follows:[12]

1. <u>No Guilt</u>. God has told us that we are to wait until marriage. Not waiting produces guilt at every level of our human interaction: with God, our partner, and with everyone else.
2. <u>No fear</u>. Waiting until marriage insures that you will never have to be afraid of contracting a sexually transmitted disease or of building a marriage on an unexpected pregnancy. In 1960 there were only two primary sexually transmitted

diseases, while today there are over twenty-seven that are commonly found in our culture. If you remain pure, there is no fear of any of these diseases entering into your relationship.

3. No comparison. Waiting until marriage insures that you will never fall into the devastating trap of comparing your spouse's sexual performance with that of a previous sexual partner. Neither will you be wondering whether you measure up to the previous partners that your spouse has had.

4. Spiritual growth. Part of the Fruit of the Spirit is self-control.[13] Waiting until marriage helps each partner to submit their physical needs and desires to the Lordship of Christ, and in the process helps them to develop self-control.

5. Greater joy. Waiting insures that there will be something saved for your marriage relationship; for that first night and for the many nights thereafter. The anticipation of the fulfillment of your relationship in sexual union is exciting. Don't spoil it by jumping the gun.

What preventative measures can you take to insure that you do not become sexually involved before marriage? The first thing to be done is to acknowledge that "marriage should be honored by all, and the marriage bed kept pure..." (Hebrews 13:5). With the Word of God as your point of reference, discuss openly with one another what physical activities should be reserved for marriage. If you have gone beyond those levels of participation, then confess that sin to God and ask Him to help you not to cross that line again before marriage.

Second, be accountable to your partner and a friend regarding this area of your life. Knowing that you will have to be open and honest with others will help you to keep this area under God's control.

Third, keep your mind pure. Just as our stomach digests and processes the things that we eat, so our mind digests and processes the things that we allow to enter it. Fill your mind with things that are good to think about; things that are pure, clean, not sexually titillating.[14] This means that you will have to personally exercise control over what you read and watch on television.

Fourth, avoid manners of dress and situations that can produce over stimulation. This may mean a change in portions of your wardrobe, and it may mean a change in the way that your dates are brought to a conclusion.

Fifth, communicate with one another regarding the struggle that you are having in this area. Together think of things that can be good substitutes for the dangerous increasing desire for physical intimacy.

Finally, ask God to help you! Sexual passion may be like a forest fire, consuming all in its path, but the apostle Paul said "I can do everything through him who gives me strength" (Philippians 4:13). In our own strength we will be destroyed by the physical passions of our bodies, but in God's strength we can be victorious and remain pure all the way to our wedding day. If you will sincerely ask God to help you, and are willing to do whatever He asks you to do, He will provide his divine enablement to help you remain pure.

"It is possible for two young people, full of all the juices that youth is endowed with by the Creator, to resist temptation. They can't do it unless they have a motive that makes it worthwhile. They can't do it alone!"[15] With all of the hormones racing through our bodies, waiting may look impossible, but with God's help this area can be carefully controlled and guided throughout the engagement period. Then with God's blessing it can be shared in all of its wonder and excitement during marriage!

QUESTIONS FOR PERSONAL REFLECTION AND COUPLE INTERACTION

1. What things do you enjoy about the current status of your physical relationship?

2. What steps are you currently taking to insure that you will come to your marriage bed pure and undefiled?

3. What additional steps, if any, do you need to add to insure that purity?

4. As your physical relationship progresses toward intercourse in marriage, what fears and apprehensions, if any, do you have ???

6

Mystery Of Love

It is often assumed that everyone knows what love is. We live in a society where the word "love" is used quite freely and applied in many different ways. The actions of our society, however, indicate that the true meaning of love is not really understood. While the song says "love makes the world go "round," it seems that crime and violence are more the case. Every day the news media reminds us of man's inhumanity to man. Almost 60% of marriages in our nation now end in divorce. Children are abused in our country at a rate that is beyond our comprehension.

It is estimated that in the entire history of the world there have been only 250 years of peace. If mankind had obeyed God's command "to love others as he has loved us"[16] the twenty billion people who have died in wars would not have died in that manner. And, in America the home would not be the most dangerous place in our nation.

One of the key figures in American psychiatry has identified what I believe is a fundamental cause of the lack of love in our culture, stating,

> "love is the medicine for our sick old world. If people can learn to give and receive love, they will usually recover from their physical or mental illness. The problem seems to be that people can't learn to receive or give love, because they don't even know how to define it. They think that it's nothing more than a warm feeling."[17]

While warm feelings toward one another are good and certainly something to be sought after, love consists of much more than elevated body temperature and perspiration on the inside of one's palms and upon one's brow.

Webster's dictionary provides, among others, two basic definitions of love. When used as a noun, it is "an affection based on admiration or benevolence . . . a warm attachment, enthusiasm, or devotion . . . unselfish concern that freely accepts another in loyalty and seeks his good." When used as a verb, it is "to hold dear . . . to feel a lover's passion, devotion, or tenderness."[18]

This provides a little help, but it still falls far short of helping the reader gain an understanding of all that love is. In order to reach that perspective, a more authoritative source must be consulted: the Bible. If we are going to understand what God says about love, then the only place to clearly see that description is in His Word.

Please read 1 Corinthians 13:3-10 and in the space below describe the quality and characteristics of Biblical love.

As you look at your relationship, is that the level of love that is present? This passage in 1 Corinthians 13 seems to be speaking about a particular level or type of love. Is that the only type of love that is to be in your relationship, or should there be some other kinds of love also present?

Today's society uses the word "love' very freely. We say we love candy bars, a certain football team, and our spouse. Within these varied contexts there are "hopefully" different shades of meaning as the word "love" is used.

The English language, while very clear and concise at times, leaves much to be desired in the fine-tuning of the word love and its varieties of meaning. The Greek language, the language of the New Testament, is, however, very helpful in seeing the specific meaning of the various uses of the word love. Three of the Greek terms translated "love" in the English usage occur in the New Testament, and a fourth term occurs in secular Greek literature.

The first word is "epithumia"; which is translated "desire, longing, craving."[19] The primary thrust of this word is the feeling that is involved, the desire that is prevalent in the relationship. It can occur in both positive and negative contexts; such as "eagerly desire"

(Luke 22:15) and "evil desire" or "lust" (2 Peter 1:4). In the marriage relationship there should certainly be a strong desire present by the partners for one another.

The second word is "phileo;" which means "to love, have affection for, to like."[20] "Phileo" love is that care and concern between good or best friends. It is being able to share everything with that special person in your life, knowing that you will be accepted as you are and your ideas and feelings not ridiculed by them.

A third New Testament word translated "love" is the word "agape."[21] This is the word that occurs most frequently in the translation "love." It is "agape" that Paul speaks of in 1 Corinthians 13, in Ephesians 5, and that John speaks of in John 3, and 1 John 4.

The fourth word that is translated "love" is "eros," from which we get the English word "erotic." Eros is that which we think of as sexual, sensual, romantic. While the Bible does not specifically use the term eros, it certainly describes this type of love and its attendant emotion in the bridegroom and bride relationship described in the Old Testament book Song of Solomon. Dr. Ed Wheat presents an excellent discussion of these four types of love in his book, <u>Love Life for Every Married Couple</u>.[22]

Epithumia, eros, and phileo love all require a positive feedback from the object of one's love. If the partner does not respond back in a similar manner, the level of intensity of the love will decrease and soon cease to exist altogether. Agape love, however, does not require a similar level of love from one's partner. Agape love is unconditional in nature and can exist by personal choice apart from private experience. One partner can exhibit agape love regardless of whether or not it is reciprocated. You can continue to express agape (sacrificial) love to your partner, even if he or she does not respond back in the same way. With this as a base, let's again consider how Paul describes love in 1 Corinthians 13:4-8a. As you look at this description of love, use it as a standard to measure the quality of your love for your fiancé.

Love is "patient" (v.4). Oops! We just started and some of us are already in trouble. What in the world is patience, other than a word in the dictionary somewhere between "pathway" and "patio?" Patience is what we wanted in our lives yesterday, so we could get on to something else today. Patience is "calm endurance," even under great affliction. This is not referring to patience with circumstances or events but with people; which is often the most difficult area in which to demonstrate it. This could be described as love "having a long fuse."

The apostle Paul said in another place, "be patient, bearing with one another in love" (Ephesians 4:2). God is patient with us; "the Lord is not slow about His promise, as some count slowness, but is patient toward you, not wishing for any to perish but for all to come to repentance" (2 Peter 3:9). I wonder how patient are we with one another. Too often we want what we want, from whom we want it, when we want it. When that does not happen, we get nervous, upset, ornery and generally "hard to get along with". What a far cry this is from the patience that is to characterize our love for others!

Love is "kind" (v.4). Kindness is showing sympathy, understanding, compassion. It is giving of oneself to benefit another, not just for friends but for enemies as well. Kindness is the complement of patience, for patience endures while kindness pays the person back with good deeds. Jesus certainly expressed kindness; "take my yoke upon you, and learn of me . . . for my yoke is easy, and my burden is light" (Matt 11:29-30). God the Father was kind toward us; demonstrated by the coming of Christ (Titus 3:4). How much kindness are you showing in your love to your partner? When your partner asks you to do something, do you say "sure, I'll be glad to do it?" Or, do you think and maybe even say, "What's in it for me?" What level of kindness are you expressing toward your mate?

Love "does not envy" (v.4). Envy is an inner boiling, seething, steaming over something that somebody else is or has. It not only says "I want what you have," but it also says "I don't want you to have it." Envy (jealousy) is a cancer, a "green-eyed monster, "that if allowed to be present will destroy any relationship. James describes it very well, "but if you harbor bitter envy and selfish ambition in your hearts, do not boast about it or deny the truth. Such wisdom does not come down from heaven but is earthly, unspiritual, of the devil. For where you have envy and selfish ambition, there you will find disorder and every evil practice" (James 3:14-16). Jealousy destroys both relationships and the people in those relationships. Agape love, that sacrificial giving love that is to be in relationships, is not jealous!

Love "does not boast" (v.4). Actually this is saying that love is not a windbag; not just a lot of "hot air". To say it another way, love is not a braggart. Once the bragging is gone there is nothing left. The one who is boastful not only builds up himself but also does it at the expense of others. Boasting is the art of "one-up-manship," the song "Anything you can do, I can do better." It is listening to what the other person is saying, all the while waiting for a chance to break in to tell them how much better you can do it. Rather than focusing all of our attention upon ourselves, love gives honor and respect to the object of our love.

Love is "not proud" (v.4). This can also be read as "love is not conceited". Pride has only one person in mind: ME. Solomon gives a clear presentation of the results of pride in the human heart; showing that it only brings shame, conflict, defeat and personal destruction.[23] Pride is like envy, a cancer that slowly eats away at the relationship and ultimately destroys it. Agape love is not proud!

Love is "not rude" (v.5). In addition to meaning "uncouth, coarse, vulgar," the word "rude" means "primitive, undeveloped".[24] It refers to not only unbecoming behavior but also to undisciplined or undeveloped behavior. To say it another way, love has developed good manners and uses them.

I am amazed and appalled at the lack of good manners that I see exhibited by people at times. Too often it seems that once a person has gotten the commitment from their spouse, they immediately forget or choose not to continue using good manners. Both men and women exhibit this tragic lack within their relationships. Love says "please," "thank you," "excuse me," and "I'm sorry." Love opens the door, takes the person's arm, helps with a coat, allows the other person to go first. Agape love continues to possess and express good manners toward the object of that love.

Love is "not self-seeking" (v.5). It is not interested only in that which will benefit himself but that which will also benefit others. It is the motive and attitude of being a servant that is presented. "For even the Son of man did not come to be served, but to serve, and to give his life as a ransom for many" (Mark 10:45). This gives us a clear picture of selflessness, of being a servant, so clearly demonstrated by the Lord Jesus Christ. It is this same selflessness, or lack of self-seeking that is to be seen in agape love within the marriage.

Love is "not easily angered" (v.5). What a contrast this is to what exists in many relationships and homes. Have you ever met a person who seemed to be walking around with "a chip on their shoulder?" It seems that they are always looking for a fight. The further and longer they walk around with that attitude, the greater the potential is that they will find a willing opponent. They will find that person who will gladly "knock it off," and the fight will immediately begin. In some relationships it seems that one or the other of the participants is looking for a fight. Since everyone has a sinful human nature, the search for someone to "do battle with" is quickly solved. They walk in the door of their home, and the conflict begins. That is not love, for love is just the opposite. Love is not looking for a fight but is looking for peace. Be a peacemaker!

Love "keeps no record of wrongs" (v.5). The phrase "to keep record" refers to a mathematical calculation, keeping count.[25] This means that love does not keep score of the wrongs that have been done so that it can then retaliate. God has separated our sins from us, as far as the east is from the west, and remembers them no more. That is exactly how we are to love one another. Things will happen in the relationship that will bring us hurt and pain, but we choose to forgive and no longer remember them. And even if we do remember, love says "that's OK, we're not keeping score." One of the reasons that some relationships are struggling is because they still keep records of things that occurred years ago. Love forgives and chooses not to remember; keeps no calculation of the wrongs that have been done.

Love "does not delight in evil" (v.6). It does not rejoice in sin; not in the sin of the individual or of their partner. Agape love does not encourage another person to sin but instead encourages them to walk with God and to live according to the principles of the Word of God.

Love "rejoices with the truth" (v.6). It determines what is the right thing to do and then does it. It knows what the right thing to say is and then says it. Love does not say the things that we think the person wants to hear, but it says the truth. And because it is said with the proper motive of care, concern, and edification, the recipient of that truth knows that it is shared in love.

For the past three verses the apostle Paul has been pounding upon the readers' hearts with his description of agape love. One would think that he was finished, but that is not so. He has five more short phrases that he uses to describe love.

Love "always protects" (v.7). Literally it means "to cover, pass over in silence, keep confidential".[26] Out of regard, respect, and honest concern for the other person, love will do everything it can to cover up and suppress the sin of that person. It does not lie and does not repress the truth but chooses not to speak about some things. Love is to be like a giant umbrella that we hold over the object of our love; to protect them from the "downpours" of this life.

A few years ago two well-known Christian Hollywood entertainers were married. The media reporters in their attempts to develop a story tried repeatedly to get the couple to speak of their sexual relationship. The comment of both partners was "we will not discuss our sexual relationship." Regardless of how extensively the reporters probed, the answer was still the same, "we will not discuss our sexual relationship." That is a good example of the "covering" or "protecting" that love does. There will be certain things in your relationship that you will keep private and not discuss with others. These are only for you and your spouse; no one else included!

Love "always trusts" (v.7). The King James Version says "love believes all things." That is a good description of this thought. Instead of being suspicious and eager to denounce the other person, love believes the best. It does not go through life cynical and suspicious. It does not quickly jump to hasty and usually erroneous conclusions. Instead, it seeks to always believe the very best about the object of their love.

Love "always hopes" (v.7). Hope is "to long for with the expectation of attainment".[27] Even in the midst of what is seemingly impossible, hope still remains. When everyone and everything else is gone, hope continues to stand by the person's side. Love does not run and leave as soon as the first mistake is made or the first sin committed. Love waits, and waits and hopes!

Love "always perseveres" (v.7). To persevere is "to persist in a state, enterprise, or undertaking in spite of influences, opposition, or discouragement."[28] To persevere is to stand one's ground in the fiercest of battles. Describing it another way, one can say that "love is not a quitter." Regardless of the opposition, regardless of the struggle, regardless of how hopeless things appear, love does not quit!

There is just one more phrase that we need to quickly look at as we consider agape love. Love "never fails" (v.8). This is not referring to success, because there are some times that love is not successful; primarily because mankind interferes with what God is seeking to do. The focus, instead, is upon it's time duration, it's permanence as a divine quality. At no time will divine (God's) love ever fail, wither, decay. By its very nature it is permanent, never to be abolished. If we have this level of love, this "agape" love, then it will continue.

Why do you love your partner? Is it because of the soft texture and beauty of their hair? The softness will turn to coarseness; the color will fade to gray and then white. And the day will come when there will be more of it left on the pillow than on your partner's head.

Is it because of his or her great physical shape? Bad news again; for our bodies change. While the coming of children brings tremendous joys into the marriage, it also makes permanent changes in a woman's body. All of the curves are still there, but they are often reshuffled and relocated a little bit. And that well-toned manly physique generally becomes less "wedge-shaped" and more "pear-shaped".

Is it because of the sweet disposition that you saw in one another? This may change as well. The pressures of work deadlines, children, medical bills and balancing busy schedules often make that loving disposition not very lovable.

People change! You are not the same person that you were one year ago and not the same person you will be one year from now. Neither is your partner! Good looks, great shapes and many other things will come to an end. We might kick, fume, fight and fuss to try to stop these things from happening. We might slow them down a little, but we will never completely prohibit their occurring.

None of those things are love. Love is what is demonstrated as those things are occurring. Love is daily expression of desire, romance, friendship, and continuing sacrificial commitment to one another.

> *"If thou must love me, let it be for naught.*
> *Except for love's sake only. Do not say*
> *'I love her for her smile--her look--her way*
> *Of speaking gently,*
> *But love me for love's sake, that evermore*
> *Thou mayest love on, through love's eternity.*[29]

QUESTIONS FOR PERSONAL REFLECTION AND COUPLE INTERACTION

1. As you look at your relationship, how would you describe the level of your love? Why do you love your fiancé?

2. To what extent is desire (epithumia) love present in your relationship? What steps can you take to keep it growing?

3. To what extent is romance (eros) love present in your relationship? What steps can you take to keep it growing?

4. To what extent is friendship (phileo) love present in your relationship? What steps can you take to keep it growing?

5. To what extent is sacrificial, total commitment (agape) love present in your relationship? What steps can you take to keep it growing?

6. 1 Corinthians 13:4-8a gives 16 descriptive phrases for agape (sacrificial) love. For each descriptive phrase indicate one practical way you can demonstrate this quality of love to your fiancé.

7

Challenge Of Understanding

Rev. Richard W. Gilbert

No skill in marriage is more important to develop than the art of clear communication. Webster has defined communication as "a process by which meanings are exchanged between individuals through a common system of symbols; a technique for expressing ideas effectively in speech or writing or through the arts."[30] Communication involves more than just the transmission of ideas or information, but also the understanding of that information by the recipient. Unless the other person has understood what has been said, communication has not really occurred. Consequently, communication involves three separate concepts: talking, listening, and understanding.

Consistent clear communication is absolutely essential to the development, growth and permanence of the marriage relationship. "The ability to communicate in mutually affirming ways is the fundamental skill which is essential to the growth of marital intimacy. Marriage provides an opportunity for multilevel exchanges of meaning. It provides the opportunity for communicating at increasingly deep levels about the things that matter most to husband and wife".[31]

Without clear communication love cannot be completely expressed and intimate knowledge of your partner cannot grow. Without clear communication problems cannot be resolved in your marriage relationship. The issue is not the possibility of communicating but the quality of the communication present.

In every marriage, communication is not a short-term goal but a life-long process. It is a never-ending highway with new and exciting challenges around each bend in the road. Because of the uncertainties present and the vulnerability required, there is a constant temptation to withdraw into individual shells or spheres of safety.

This withdrawal does not facilitate communication but instead fractures it. If true, open, dynamic, growing communication is going to occur in a couple's relationship, it will occur only as the individual members risk being open to and known by one another. The more open that you are with one another during your engagement period, the more solid will be the foundation of love upon which you build your marriage.

Levels of Communication

Communication occurs in relationships on many levels. John Powell, in his book <u>Why Am I Afraid to Tell You Who I Am?</u>, states that we communicate on at least five different levels, extending from shallow clichés to sincere honesty and understanding of feelings.[32] Following are Powell's five levels of communication:

Level Five: <u>Clichés</u>. Here phrases are uttered more from habit than meaning. One might hear at this level, "How are you doing?", "Have a nice day," "Nice to see you." There is no personal sharing, and no real intent to listen to any response that the other person might offer to one of these comments. Communication at this level is "at arm's length" and accidental at best.

Level Four: <u>Reporting the Facts About Others</u>. Conversation at this level is like listening to the six o'clock news: pure information. At this level one would hear, "Jim got a new job," "The temperature is two degrees below zero," "There are storm clouds in the sky this morning." At this level we offer no personal commentary on these facts, and there is nothing indicated about how we feel regarding these things.

Level Three: <u>My Ideas and Judgments</u>. Here the person is willing to share his ideas, judgments, decisions. At this level the person is beginning to lower the defensive barriers and make himself open and vulnerable to others. The individual communicating at this level might say, "I think it is going to storm today," "If you go out in that cold weather, you might get frostbite on your fingers," "You sure have a pretty smile."

Level Two: <u>My Feelings or Emotions</u>. At this level the person expresses how he feels about the facts, ideas, and judgments that have already been shared. These are the feelings that are uniquely him. Many more of the defensive barriers are removed here, and the individual's heart is laid open before those to whom he is talking.

Level One: <u>Peak Communication</u>. Here there is understanding of the other person's feelings and emotions. "I understand that seeing her act that way makes you feel sad." "Your comment just now shows me that you are happy about what happened."

According to Powell we communicate with one another at these five different levels. We do not always communicate with one another at the same level. On some issues we will restrict our communication to one or two levels, while on other issues we will work our way through all five levels. The better we know a person, the more our communication will move from level five (clichés) toward levels three through one. During the engagement period, there should be consistent increasing communication at every level.

As has already been indicated, communication is something that is constantly occurring. The question that must be continually asked and answered is not whether we will communicate, but what will be the quality of that communication.

Hindrances in Communication

While communication can be improving in a relationship, at times there will be hindrances to that improvement. Some hindrances to good communications in our interpersonal relationships follow.

First being too quick to speak is a hindrance. Most people prefer to speak rather than to listen. Too often a response is given before the other person has even completed sharing their thought or idea. Proverbs 18:13 says, "He who answers before listening that is his folly and his shame."

Second, talking too much is a hindrance. Here one person dominates the conversation, not being sensitive to the other person's need to speak. Generally, this occurs because the person believes that what they have to say is the most important. Ecclesiastes 5:2 says, "Do not be quick with your mouth, do not be hasty in your heart to utter anything before God. God is in heaven and you are on earth, so let your words be few."

Third, the silent treatment, not talking enough, is a hindrance. Here one person may feel that he has nothing of value to share, or that talking about the matter will not make any difference. Consequently he says nothing at all or only enough "to get by." Too often what this communicates is lack of interest or even anger toward the other person. Ecclesiastes 3:7 says, There is "a time to tear and a time to mend, a time to be silent and a time to speak."

Fourth, blame shifting is a hindrance. The individual refuses to accept any responsibility for what has occurred and points the finger of guilt at others. Galatians 5:15 states, "If you keep on biting and devouring each other, watch out or you will be destroyed by each other." Colossians 3:12-13 says, "Therefore, as God's chosen people, holy and dearly loved, clothe yourselves with compassion, kindness, humility, gentleness and patience. Bear with each other and forgive whatever grievances you may have against one another. Forgive as the Lord forgave you."

Fifth, arguments and anger are hindrances to good interpersonal communication. These are like sandpaper that rub raw the surface of the relationship. When one person is angry, he is generally not willing to listen to the words and feelings of another. When one has been wounded by the words of another, he is not quickly receptive to more words from that person. Several Proverbs give us additional insight:

> "An offended brother is more unyielding than a fortified city, and disputes are like the barred gates of a citadel" (Proverbs 18:19).

> "A man of knowledge uses words with restraint, and a man of understanding is even-tempered" (Proverbs 17:27).

> "A man's wisdom gives him patience; it is to his glory to overlook an offense" (Proverbs 19:11).

Elements of God Communication

It is not enough to identify those things that are hindrances to good communication. In addition, it is necessary to indicate and describe some of the elements of good communication. If communication is going to improve in any relationship, it must include the following elements.

First, honesty must be present. Be absolutely truthful in all of your interpersonal communication. It is amazing how often people are selective in their truthfulness with one another. Many relationships have ended because of the lack of total honesty between the participants. Proverbs 19:5 states, "A false witness will not go unpunished, and he who pours out lies will not go free." Proverbs 26:28 adds, "A lying tongue hates those it hurts, and a flattering mouth works ruin."

Second, forgiveness must be present. Forgiveness is to no longer hold against the other person a word, action, or thought which they have exhibited toward you. It does not mean that it did not happen, nor does it mean that it no longer surfaces in your mind. It does mean that when it comes to your attention, you <u>choose</u> to no longer think about it and allow it to affect your relationship with that person.

Third, trust is an essential element. This is an assured reliance on the character, ability, strength or truth of the other person. It is knowing that they will act in your best interest and not violate the confidentiality which exists between you. Proverbs 17:9 states, "He who covers over an offense promotes love, but whoever repeats the matter separates close friends."

Fourth, acceptance is essential. Accept the other person as they are, not as you want them to become. An unconditional relationship promotes good communication, while a conditional one hinders it. Romans 15:7 says, "Accept one another, then, just as Christ accepted you, in order to bring praise to God."

Finally, patience is required. Every person is still <u>under construction</u>; none are yet perfect. Consequently, it is absolutely vital that we remember the phrase, "Please be patient; God is not finished with me yet." Proverbs 15:18 states, "A hot-tempered man stirs up dissension, but a patient man calms a quarrel."

We have presented some of the hindrances to and elements of good communication between individuals. Another question needs to be raised at this time, and that is "What are some of the things that couples need to talk about during the engagement period?'. Actually this question can be answered in one word: <u>everything</u>!

Many couples have come into my office for premarital counseling, believing that they had already discussed everything possible. Once the counseling sessions began, however, they soon realized that they had only begun to talk about some of the issues, while other issues were being quietly and carefully avoided.

Following is a short list of some of the things that need to be discussed during the engagement period.

1. Where will you live?
2. Who is going to work?
3. Who is going to continue their education?
4. Who is responsible for the household duties?
5. Who will handle the finances?
6. Where will the honeymoon be, and how much will you spend?
7. Are you going to have children?
8. When and how many children will you have?
9. What method of birth control will you use?
10. Where will you go to church?
11. How active are you going to be in church?
12. How often will you visit your parents?
13. With what friends will you socialize?
14. What types of leisure activities will you have?
15. Who will use the the car (if only one)?
16. How will you divide up the household chores?
17. Where will you spend the holidays?

These questions just barely "scratch the surface" of the areas that need to be discussed during the engagement period. Every area of human life, every area of your relationship needs to be openly, honestly, carefully talked about.

As you join together in marriage you begin a communication process that will last your entire lifetime. It is a process that you will have to work at. It will not come easy! There will be many times that you will be ready to throw up your hands in frustration and cry out "What's the use." Don't give up! Continue to talk and listen responsively. Express opposing ideas lovingly and listen to opposing ideas openly.

While much more could be said, the above material will help

you to build a solid foundation of communication in your marriage. What remains for you to do is to PRACTICE-PRACTICE-PRACTICE. The more you strive toward good communication at every level, the more proficient you will become. It is not enough for you to know the information. What is now required is its application in your relationship.

QUESTIONS FOR PERSONAL REFLECTION AND COUPLE INTERACTION

1. Consider Powell's five levels of communication. At what level do you find that you and your partner spend most of the time communicating?

2. At what level would you like to communicate, and what steps can you take to make that a reality?

3. Which of you communicates most easily? Why?

4. What are some of the hindrances in your communication? What steps can be taken to break these barriers down?

5. What are some of the strengths of your communication?

6. Are you always honest in your communication with one another? Why or why not?

7. At times, do you find it difficult to concentrate without being easily distracted when your partner is speaking to you? Why? What are three steps that you can take to change this?

8. How do you know if your fiancé really hears what you are saying?

9. What are some aspects of your relationship that you have not discussed or are apprehensive about discussing? What steps can you take to change this?

10. With the help of a Bible concordance, look up and read together all of the verses in Proverbs that speak of the tongue and our words.

8

Energizing Emotions

Webster defines emotions as "the affective aspect of consciousness-feeling; a psychic and physical reaction subjectively experienced as strong feeling and physiologically involving changes that prepare the body for immediate vigorous action."[33]

Emotions are subjectively experienced and may result in overt objective consequent behavior. Emotions may be merely felt, or they may be acted upon in our personal lives. A young man may say to his fiancee, "I love you" and sense within himself that warm attendant sensation in his stomach and chest. Or, he may take these emotions the next step and kiss her tenderly and softly.

Emotions can run from one end of the descriptive continuum to the other; from very positive to very negative. Some positive emotions are joy, excitement, anticipation, love. Some negative emotions are depression, rejection, fear, anxiety, loneliness, disappointment, sorrow and anger.

One of the most exciting (an emotion) challenges of your marriage will be to identify and understand the emotions that your partner is experiencing. If your partner had a neon sign across his chest that flashed the descriptive word for the emotion he was currently experiencing, it would be a great help. But, that does not happen! Instead, the way that he responds may indicate any number of possible emotions. One of your tasks in marriage will be to understand what your partner is feeling, his/her emotions, and then respond appropriately.

Within themselves, many emotions are neither right nor wrong. They are merely an indication of what is happening in the person. They are like a thermostat that measures the amount of heat. The thermostat does not cause the heat or affect it in any direction but only measures its presence. Emotions function similarly in conjunction with the person's inner being.

It is very important to understand that emotions are God-given. When God made Adam, He built into the person of this new creation a variety of different emotions. God had said "let us make man in our image, in our likeness . . ."[34]. That does not mean that

God has physical attributes like mankind does. Instead, it means that man has personality, just as God has personality.

A variety of definitions could be given to describe personality. Personality was at one time described as consisting of knowledge, emotion, and will. A more complete description includes life, purpose, freedom, intelligence, activity, self-consciousness, spirituality and emotion.

God has all of these characteristics of personhood, including emotions. God is jealous (Deut. 5:9), grieved (Judges 10:16), compassionate (Psalm 103:13), joyous (Isaiah 62:5), loving (Jeremiah 31:3) and angry (Romans 1:18). Since God is absolutely pure and holy, there is no sin in any of these emotional components of God's nature.

Because man is made in the image of God, part of that image is his emotional makeup. By the creative act of God, man was shaped, formed, and placed on this earth with emotions. God's evaluation of mankind's creation was, "it was very good."[35]

When mankind disobeyed God in the Garden of Eden, a new component came onto the scene: sin. What was previously pure and holy was now distorted by the ugliness of sin, and that includes mankind's emotions. This does not mean that man's emotions are sinful and should be avoided. Instead, it means that even at their very best and purest form, they still fall short of God's standard of perfection. Man will never be able to express his emotions at their purest level until he is in heaven. Until then, man's sinful nature will constantly effect the possession and expression of his emotions.

In your marriage there will be joys, depressions, excitement, anger, fears, tensions and many other emotions that each of you will individually face. Some of these will be shared with one another, and some of these will be faced alone. Part of the task in marriage is not to conform your partner's emotions to your own but instead to understand them. Only then can you help your partner respond in a godly, obedient way.

Rev. Richard W. Gilbert

Anger

While a wide spectrum of emotions impact interpersonal relationships both positively and negatively, the one that generally causes the most difficulty is anger. One partner may describe what they are feeling as a small difficulty, a little tension, some frustration, but what is really present is anger.

There are many ways that anger can be described. The simplest definition of anger is "an emotional reaction of extreme displeasure."[36] This emotional reaction often interferes in the communication process between the two partners.

Some of the anger that people experience is good, some bad, some justified, some unjustified. There are a number of ways in which people traditionally respond to the presence of anger in their lives:

1. They "blow off steam." They open their mouths and virtually exercise no control over what is said.
2. They delude themselves. They say, "I am not angry;" while all the while sitting there with teeth gritting and fists clenched.
3. They fire "zingers". Here they concentrate on saying caustic comments to their partner.
4. They shift the blame. They refuse to acknowledge any personal complicity in what has occurred. It is all the other person's fault.
5. They become mute. They will not talk about it but instead prefer to keep it "bottled up" inside of themselves.

These methods of resolving anger have the same end result: the anger is not corrected but instead becomes more entrenched. It is like a splinter of wood that has gotten into your hand. Unless it is removed, it will fester and the wound will become much more serious.

At different times God was angry with mankind, and since God is holy and sinless then his anger must have been justified.[37] Since God's anger is always correct, then there must be times when our anger is also correct, justifiable. One of the major dilemmas for us as Christians is determining when our anger is justifiable. How can we know when it is OK to feel this way? Anger is justifiable when it is directed against sin and its results. We should be angry about pornography, child abuse, abortion, adultery and many other things that are clearly the open operation of sin in this world. God is angry at these things, and we also should have a righteous anger toward them.

There is also an anger that comes when our plans are frustrated or when we are treated insensitively. At times the anger we experience resulting from these circumstances is also justifiable. As a general rule, if the anger we are experiencing does not fall into the above categories, then we can be fairly certain that it is not justifiable.

How is the believer to respond to anger? How can you biblically handle this intense emotion in your personal life and relationships? God has not left you without direction in this matter but has provided a standard for evaluation and steps for resolution. The Bible speaks directly to this matter in several passages:

> "Refrain from anger and turn from wrath; do not fret--it leads only to evil" (Psalm 37:8).

> "A quick-tempered man does foolish things, and a crafty man is hated" (Proverbs 14:17).

> "A gentle answer turns away wrath, but a harsh word stirs up anger" (Proverbs 15:1).

> "Do not make friends with a hot-tempered man, do not associate with one easily angered, or you may learn his ways and get yourself ensnared" (Proverbs 22:24-25).

"In your anger do not sin; do not let the sun go down while you are still angry . . . Do not let any unwholesome talk come out of your mouths, but only what is helpful for building others up according to their needs, that it may benefit those who listen . . . Get rid of all bitterness, rage and anger, brawling and slander, along with every form of malice" (Ephesians 4:26, 29, 31).

"My dear brothers, take note of this: Everyone should be quick to listen, slow to speak and slow to become angry, for man's anger does not bring about the righteous life that God desires" (James 1:19-20).

There are several positive steps that can be taken for resolution of anger in your interpersonal relationships. First, be aware of and admit your emotions. Denying that you are angry will not make the anger go away. If you are going to correct the problem, you must first admit that there is a problem.

Second, try to identify the source or cause of your anger. Identification of the cause will enable you to take steps to remove it. You may be surprised at what you find here!

Third, tell your partner that you are angry. They can already see the change that has occurred in your demeanor. This will begin to set the stage for discussion of the issue.

Fourth, focus attention upon the act that was done, not on the person who committed the act. God hates the sin that is done, but He does not hate the sinner. Too often when we are angry we focus our attention in the wrong place: upon the person. Nothing is accomplished by this misplaced focus. Positive resolution will come only as we focus upon the act!

Fifth, deal with the anger as soon as possible. Address and resolve the matter if possible before the next day begins. If that is not an option, then set a time within the next day or two for further discussion.

Finally, pray individually and together as a couple about the issue. All of the steps taken to this point will still ultimately fail without God's enablement. By placing the matter in God's hands, final blocks to healing will be removed.

Man, who has been made in the image of God, has a wide range of emotions that are for the enrichment of his life. How he uses them is his decision. He can either control them or be controlled by them. It is these very emotions, given to enrich your life, that will ultimately fill your marriage and all your personal relationships with the joy, vibrancy and life that God wants to be there.

QUESTIONS FOR PERSONAL REFLECTION AND COUPLE INTERACTION

1. How would you describe your emotions over the past week? Over the past month?

2. How would you describe your partner's emotions over the past week? Over the past month?

3. What is your greatest emotional need? Your partner's?

4. How well do you express your emotions to your partner?

5. How well do you sense and understand your partner's emotions? Which emotion(s) do you readily see and understand? Which do you have the most difficulty seeing and understanding?

6. What steps can you take to provide a safe environment for and assist your partner in sharing his or her emotions?

7. What types of things or situations cause you to become angry?

8. How do you normally respond to the presence of anger in your life? In your partner's life?

9. Think of a recent situation in which you did not handle anger well. What could you have done differently to improve the outcome?

9

Resolving Conflicts In Marriage

As you read the title, you may be saying to yourself, "what is he talking about? My partner and I love one another. We get along perfectly and are in complete harmony with one another. We have not disagreed on anything, and we don't expect that to change. We are going to become one, and that means that we will <u>always</u> be in harmony with one another."

Well, while these are admirable thoughts and certainly a worthwhile target to aim at, the possibility of this becoming a reality is non-existent. God is bringing together in your home two separate individuals, with two distinct and separate personalities. You are becoming one, but you are still continuing your uniqueness that makes each of you a separate person. Each of you needs someone who can complement you; not a carbon copy of yourself. You need one who "fills the void," satisfies your deepest needs.

Since you are separate people, there will be times when some level of conflict between you will be inevitable. There will be times when you will not agree about things. Personal feelings will not be taken into consideration and one of you will, at times, be hurt through the intentional or unintentional acts and words of your partner.

There will be times when your partner will not agree with you about certain issues. There will be problems that arise which will need to be addressed and worked out. This is not something that is isolated to your relationship, but it is a normal part of the process of two people adapting to one another and building a growing marriage unit.

None of the problems and conflicts that you experience are impossible to resolve. None of them have to threaten the security of your relationship. None of them have to be the cause for the dissolution of your marriage. Every conflict area of your relationship can be examined, resolved, and permanent healing provided. As you work together as a couple in the healing-resolution process, your relationship as a couple is stretched and strengthened. While conflict can be detrimental if ignored or improperly handled, it can also be a tremendous opportunity for growth in a relationship. The determining factor is how you respond to it.

Basic Principles

Suggestions have been made by various authors regarding basic principles of conflict resolution.[38] While there are many views regarding the corrective measures to be taken, the following appear to be the basic principles for conflict resolution. First, begin with a commitment to your relationship and a commitment to work things out. If you do not have this as a starting point, you will not be ready and willing to do the difficult things that resolution may require.

Second, address the conflict issue in private, not out in the public forum. This is a private issue between the two of you and should be handled accordingly.

Third, verbal dialogue is a must. Nothing can be accomplished by one of you refusing to discuss the matter.

Fourth, having begun the conversation, state those areas in which you agree. This helps you to see the firm basis upon which you will be building.

Fifth, sincerely try to see the issue from your partner's point of view. There is always more than one way to perceive a matter. Just beginning to see the issue from your partner's perspective may change your personal position.

Sixth, address the issue, not the person. It is not the inner person that we are having the conflict with; it is the action that has been done. Focusing upon the issue maintains the integrity and self-image of the persons involved; providing a safe arena for disagreement.

Seventh, keep an open mind. Pre-conceptions terminate meaningful, constructive communication. An open mind, however, is the catalyst that can generate clear and accurate solutions.

Eighth, talk things through to their conclusion. If communication regarding the matter is only partially completed, then the matter will only be partially resolved.

Ninth, be willing to admit your error and forgive your partner. If you are wrong then admit it and ask your partner's forgiveness. If your partner is in error, then be quick to forgive him and then set the matter behind you. Then deliberately choose to no longer think about that matter.

Finally, pray about those areas in which you have conflict. We are exhorted repeatedly throughout the New Testament to pray about matters.[39] Every conflict in your interpersonal relationship can be resolved with God's help! It is through prayer that you are seeking that help from God.

Specific Steps

Now, with these ten principles of conflict resolution in mind, how can you address and work through a specific area of conflict. The following general steps can be applied in almost every area of interpersonal conflict. First, identify the area or specific issue of conflict. Nothing can be resolved until you both agree upon exactly what the issues are.

Second, be honest about your individual part in the conflict. Just as "it takes two to tango", it takes two to have a conflict.

Third, think of a number of possible ways that this conflict could be resolved. The best approach here is "brainstorming;" any and every possible solution is recorded.

Fourth, from this list eliminate those things that have already been tried and have not worked.

Fifth, from the list select one untried possible solution and individually commit yourself to working on that solution for the next week.

Sixth, at the end of the week evaluate your progress. If progress has been made, then continue efforts in the same direction. If progress has not been made, then select a different possible solution and begin working on that.

Finally, when the conflict has been resolved, then celebrate the success. Each celebration is an encouragement for the next series of conflict resolution steps. Since you worked through other problems, then you can certainly work through this one!

Conflict in a relationship is not something bad; something to be avoided. It is an inevitable product of two different people getting to know and interact with one another. With each conflict examined, addressed, and resolved the couple's relationship is further strengthened.

In the early 1980's, while attending school in northern Indiana, I frequently drove by a foundry in our town. On occasion, the building's outer doors near the blast furnace would be open. This allowed a view of the giant cauldron containing the liquid iron ore, with the fire burning under it. The constant high temperature of the fire under the cauldron caused the impurities in the iron ore to boil to the surface. These impurities were then "skimmed off" the top, and the resulting metal produced was much stronger than the ore at the beginning of the process.

That is what conflict does in a relationship. It brings to the surface those areas of struggle, differences, "impurities". As they are addressed and "skimmed-off", the result is something that is much purer and stronger than was present before.

QUESTIONS FOR PERSONAL REFLECTION
AND COUPLE INTERACTION

1. What issues or areas of conflict currently exist in your relationship?

2. What was the last conflict issue that you worked through in your couple relationship?

3. What steps did you take in resolving it? What was the end result? Were you each satisfied with the result? Why? Why not? What would you do (if anything) to change the result?

4. What part should prayer have in conflict resolution? What part did it play in your last conflict as a couple? How can you make it a greater part in future conflicts you will have?

5. Read and summarize these passages: Ephesians 6:18; Philippians 4:6-7; 1 Thessalonians 5:17; James 4:2-3; 1 Peter 5:7.

10

Wise Management
Of God's Money

The issue of finances is one of the greatest potential areas for satisfaction or conflict within the marriage. While each couple's goal should be to achieve a deep personal satisfaction resulting from being a good steward, improper financial management or lack of agreement on financial responsibilities between marriage partners will quickly produce intense tension. Since the proper handling of this area can actually eliminate numerous arguments and periods of anguishing frustration, it is critical that we carefully address this subject.

While most couples have heard repeatedly about the necessity of having a budget, knowing where their money is being spent, there are still a large number who do not have an operational budget for their homes. Many working couples find that after the bills are paid they have no money left for savings. Many couples are being consumed by spiraling credit card debt. Most recent estimates in 2020 show the average credit card debt in the United States to be $6,200 per family. Some have two or more credit cards; borrowing to the maximum limit on each card; paying annual interest rates from thirteen to thirty percent on those debts.

Many working couples have no idea how much they are really spending and think that they are bringing home more money than they actually are. Some couples lose all sense of financial responsibility, spending two to three times beyond their monthly income. Some couples would like to go to one income, allowing the wife to remain at home with the family, but their current monthly income compared to their indebtedness eliminates that possibility.

The Word of God does not say that money is the root of evil. Instead it says that the "<u>love</u> of money is a root of all kinds of evil".[40] The issue is not possession but our attitudes toward possession. Continuing to describe the effect of loving money, Paul says "Some people, eager for money, have wandered from the faith and pierced themselves with many griefs."[41] A five minute examination of the daily news will show the depths to which mankind will go to satisfy his <u>love</u> for money. Countless lives, Christian and non-Christian alike, have been destroyed by the continual reach for more and more money.

In some families dual work and dual incomes are a matter of necessity, while in others they are a matter of choice. Because of societal pressure and the constant demand for more things, the debt level in some households has rapidly increased, forcing both partners into the work field. In many communities the steady increase in government costs, passed on to the public in taxes, has had the same impact upon the family. In some families the inability to say "No" to purchases has either forced both partners into the work place or increased the number of working hours for the one currently employed.

For a couple to be able to wisely manage the finances which they have at their disposal, they must see those finances through God's eyes. They must have a biblical view of finances.

There is one basic principle, which, if understood and adhered to, will revolutionize the way that you perceive your material resources. That principle simply stated is, "God owns everything in this world!" The following two Scripture passages illustrate this principle;

> "The earth is the Lord's and everything in it, the world, and all who live in it" (Psalm 24:1).

> "Yours, O Lord, is the greatness and the power and the glory and the majesty and the splendor, for everything in heaven and earth is yours. Yours, O Lord, is the kingdom; you are exalted as head over all...Everything comes from you, and we have given you only what comes from your hand" (1 Chronicles 29:11, 14b).

Everything that we have and use does not really belong to us but instead to God. We are given the privilege of using these items, but they are not really ours. We are, in reality, property managers. What God expects us to be is <u>good</u> property managers.

It does not matter how much money you possess, but it is instead the attitude that you demonstrate toward that money that is important. It is our attitude toward our possessions that concerns God. The resources that God provides are to be used and enjoyed but not greedily sought after.[42] He has given us all things to enjoy[43], and it is our duty to keep them in the right perspective in our hearts.

Purpose of Money

Since God owns everything, and we are merely managing that which he entrusts to our care, we must ask the question, "What is the purpose of money or material resources?" The answer to this question can be quite definitive and detailed as some theologians have done.[44] Or, it can be quite general in nature, which will be the approach here.

Basically there are four purposes for money or material resources. First, to provide for individual and family needs. "If anyone does not provide for his relatives, and especially for his immediate family, he has denied the faith and is worse than an unbeliever" (1 Timothy 5:8).

Second, to assist others with their needs. "If anyone has material possessions and sees his brother in need but has no pity on him, how can the love of God be in him? Dear children, let us not love with words or tongue but with actions and in truth" (1 John 3:17-18).

Third, to reach others with the gospel. "Selling their possessions and goods, they gave to anyone as he had need . . . And the Lord added to their number daily those who were being saved" (Acts 2:45, 47).

Fourth, to enjoy God's blessings. "Command those who are rich in this present world not to be arrogant nor to put their hope in wealth, which is so uncertain, but to put their hope in God, who richly provides us with everything for our enjoyment."

Money Management Principles

Since everything that we possess is given to us by God, to be enjoyed, to be used to meet our needs and the needs of others, and to reach the world with the gospel, then there is an additional area that must be examined. How can those resources best be utilized? Following are some practical hints that have been gleaned through the years, both from personal experience and from the godly counsel of others. These principles have helped us to live through times of "plenty" and through times of "want."

First, be able to distinguish between needs, wants and desires. Advertising has one primary purpose: to stimulate a desire in you to purchase something that you really don't need. A quick check of closets, drawers and garages will show how effective that advertising has been. Basic needs are food, clothes, a home, health care, a job. Wants are comforts, conveniences; things a little nicer than is really necessary. Desires, on the other hand, are luxuries; items you can get along without. For example, a need might be a used Ford, a want might be a year old Buick, while a desire would be a new Corvette. Or, a need might be a meal of rice and beans, a want would be a steak, and a desire would be eating out often.

Second, always agree together on expenditures. Discussion does not have to occur for each purchase, but the general budget allotment in that area should have been discussed. One couple related that they had agreed never to spend over $10.00 on any item without their partner's agreement. This is a very good principle to put into effect immediately in your marriage.

Third, never purchase anything on impulse. You'll be surprised how few things you really need, especially after you have had twenty-four hours to think about it. Avoid the urge of instant gratification, for it generally leads to long-term payments.

Fourth, avoid the credit system as much as possible. A general principle here is "purchase only what you have the money to pay for." There should only be two things that you purchase on credit:

transportation and housing. Because of the high price of homes, it is necessary to have a mortgage. Transportation is another matter, and you should work toward the day when you can purchase a vehicle with cash.

You may need to secure one credit card in order to establish a credit rating. There are advantages to having a credit card: for emergencies, identification, tax records and the ability to write checks. If you use the credit card for a purchase, be sure that you have the money in the bank to pay off the bill when it comes. A credit card can be very helpful, but it can also bring financial suicide if abused. The <u>very best</u> rule is "owe no man anything."[45]

Fifth, be systematic in your finances. There is no need to wrestle with your finances more than once or twice a month. Keeping adequate records and a checking account are absolutely necessary for organized and sensible handling of your funds.

Sixth, give systematically of your resources to God. Give of the first of your possessions, not the last. Give with a heart that overflows with love to God; thanking Him for the privilege of giving.[46] Give to God the tithe and an offering above that!

Finally, have a budget. The only way to be certain of what is coming in and what is going out is to prepare a budget; accounting in detail for what is spent and then deciding what should be spent to meet financial goals.

A budget is indispensable for every couple. It will help set goals for spending, saving, investing and giving, and will help in evaluating progress toward achieving those goals. It will put you in control of the money, not vice-versa. It will help you become more faithful stewards of the money that God has entrusted into your care.[47]

Make your budget work for you, not you working for it. It is to be your slave, not your master. Be somewhat flexible, but be able to corporately assess your financial position so that you know what is within range of affordability for you. One Christian financial counselor has given the following rule of thumb for financial disbursement:[48] Housing (32% of net income), food

(15%), automobiles (15%), debts (5%), insurance (5%), recreation-entertainment (7%), clothing (5%), medical-dental expenses (5%), savings (5%), miscellaneous (6%). This is an <u>ideal</u> distribution that may be far from your current circumstances. For personal financial freedom, begin today to work toward this distribution.

There are many excellent resources available to help you carefully and wisely manage the money that God has given you. A number of these are noted in the bibliography in the back of this book. A budget worksheet is included in Appendix B.

QUESTIONS FOR PERSONAL REFLECTION AND COUPLE INTERACTION

1. Do you have a personal budget that you are currently using?

2. Who is going to work?

3. Do you plan to buy or rent a dwelling?

4. What is your opinion of buying on credit? Are you currently in debt? If so, how long at the current payment rate will it take to pay off that debt?

5. How much money do you think will be needed to run your household?

6. How will you determine how the money is spent? Who will write the checks?

7. How much money should be allocated to the following areas:

   Personal expenses (allowances)?
   Recreational activities?
   Contributions?
   Savings?

8. If the wife does work and becomes pregnant, how will the family adjust to the lower income?

9. How do you feel about the way your partner handles money? How do you feel about the way you handle money? How does your partner feel about the way you handle money?

10. Identify and list three financial goals for your marriage: for the first year; for the first five years.

11. Please turn to Appendice B and fill out the budget sheet for your life together as a couple; beginning with your wedding day.

11

Family Relationships

When a man and a woman agree to be marriage partners they bring into that relationship more than themselves. They also bring two sets of parents, and even more if divorce and remarriage has been there in one or both families. For the couple to say that their spouse's parents are not going to have an effect upon their marriage is like an ostrich "sticking its head in the sand." The only way that in-laws will have no effect on the couple's relationship is if the newly weds immediately move to the interior of Antarctica, have no contact of any kind with the outside world, and the parents have no idea where they have gone. As long as the couple's parents are alive, through their communication and interaction they will impact this new family unit. What the couple must address and determine is the level and quality of that interaction.

You are now establishing a home of your own, and of necessity your relationship with your parents is changing. After eighteen to twenty years of living in their homes, the nature of the parent-child relationship is being drastically modified. When you marry you are no longer directly accountable to your parents, yet there is an emotional bond and interaction pattern that will continue for the duration of your lives. During this modification process, tremendous strain is often put on all parties involved. When one of those parties resists the change, it serves only to intensify the strain that already exists. As a result many sons, daughters, and sometimes even parents are frustrated; not knowing what to do to bring harmony into the tense relationship.

When you marry you do not cease to be the son or daughter of your parents. You will always be that! You are still to honor your mother and father for as long as you live, but you are no longer accountable to "obey them." Listen to what they have to say, thank them for their advice, and then make your own decision in light of all of the available evidence. Your relationship becomes more like that which you have with a close friend.

It is necessary to remember that this change in relationship will not be an immediate occurrence but will require much time! It is best to begin this change in the relationship long before the marriage occurs, so that the adjustment process will have already begun by the time the wedding vows are said.

The engagement period is short when compared to the lifetime of your marriage. During this short period of time, it is absolutely essential for you to begin to talk about your families and the types of things that occurred in your individual homes. The topics for open communication are unlimited. You will not be able to talk about everything; that will take the rest of your life to accomplish. The engagement period is just the beginning!

The following guidelines for relating to one's in-laws have been suggested by Landis and Landis.[49] Every couple would do well to refresh their memory of these from time to time.

1. Treat your in-laws with the same consideration and respect you give to friends who are not in-laws.
2. When in-laws take an interest in your life and give advice, do just as you would if any friend gave advice; if it is good, follow it, if it is not good, accept it graciously and then ignore it.
3. Remember that many times when the in-laws appear to be too concerned with your affairs, they are not trying to interfere in your life but are sincerely interested in your welfare.
4. Look for the good points in your in-laws.
5. When visiting your in-laws, make the visits reasonably short.
6. When visiting in-laws, be as thoughtful, courteous, and helpful as you are when you are visiting other friends.
7. Accept your in-laws as they are; remember that they would probably like to make changes in you, too.
8. Mothers-in-law have been close to their children before marriage; give them time to find new interests in life.

9. Go into marriage with a positive attitude toward your in-laws. You believe it is a good family to marry into, and you intend to enjoy your new family.
10. Give advice to your in-laws only if they ask for it; even then, use self-restraint.
11. Discuss the faults of your partner only with him or her, not with your family.
12. Do not quote your family or hold them up as models to your partner.
13. Remember, it takes at least two people to create an in-law problem. No one person is ever entirely to blame.

In addition to the above guidelines, these additional thoughts should be considered. Establish a genuine friendship with your in-laws. Look for common areas of interest; things that you can do together as families. Preserve a healthy independence from them, regardless of how close you live to them and how much time you spend interacting as families. Keep tension and strife to a minimum around sensitive areas. Some issues, such as money, children, politics, and possibly even religion, are better avoided in discussion.

Holidays are often an especially difficult time for new couples. One possible way to handle this is to visit one set of parents on one holiday and the other parents on another holiday. When you go to your parent's home, keep your time there short. Family traditions do not have to be passed down from generation to generation. Begin your <u>own</u> traditions as a couple!

Finally, keep in mind that you, too, will probably be a parent-in-law someday. So, do unto others as you wish them to some day do unto you!

QUESTIONS FOR PERSONAL REFLECTION
AND COUPLE INTERACTION

Family and Social Background

1. As a child, what did you enjoy most about your family?

2. As a child, how important were birthdays, anniversaries and holidays in your family?

3. What degree of happiness or unhappiness existed in your parent's home while you were growing up?

4. How did your parents resolve the conflicts that sometimes were present between them?

5. How often was conflict present in your home?

6. How did you respond to the way your parents resolved their conflicts?

7. Has divorce occurred in your family?

8. What is your present relationship with members of your immediate family? Your extended family?

Family Interaction

1. As you look at your fiancé's family, are you excited or apprehensive about being a part of it? Why?

2. Do you want your marriage to be like that of your parents or in-laws? Why or why not?

3. What positive qualities do you see in your parents? In your in-laws?

4. What negative qualities do you see in your parents? In your in-laws?

5. How do your parents view you? Your in-laws?

6. How near do you plan to live to your parents (both sets)?

7. How much time do you feel you will want to spend with your parents?

8. How will you spend holidays and other times of family gathering?

9. If a conflict exists between one set of parents and you as a couple, who should handle it? Why?

12

Daily Living

Rev. Richard W. Gilbert

A number of years ago I walked into a lapidary shop in the town in which I was living. In the front of the shop was a cement mixer, with plastic sealing it's open front. Inside the mixer were a number of small to medium size rocks; a liquid solution covered the rocks. The machine was running; causing the rocks to tumble against one another. The store owner explained that the machine was "polishing" the rocks. The "rough" rocks were placed in the mixer, an oil and water solution added, the opening sealed, and the mixer turned on. The mixer would run continuously for the next 30 days, during which time the oil and water would keep the rocks lubricated while they constantly knocked against one another. Slowly over that time period the rough edges would be chipped, worn down and smoothed. At the end of the process the rocks would be less jagged, closer fitting to one another, smoother, and polished.

That is a fairly good description of what happens in marriage. Daily living in marriage is like a cement mixer in which the husband and wife are present, with the water of commitment, and the oil of love. As they continuously knock against one another, the jagged protrusions are chipped off, the "rough" edges smoothed. This smoothing, polishing, process daily fits them closer and closer to one another.

It is to this daily process of living that I would like to direct your attention in this chapter. The material will be divided into three topical areas: physical health; housing, education, employment; and recreation-leisure time.

Physical Health

David said that God formed us and wove us together while we were in our mother's womb. He said that "I am fearfully and wonderfully made; your works are wonderful, I know that full well" (Psalm 130:14). The human body is an amazing complex machine designed by God; constructed never to wear out, to live forever. However, when Adam and Eve sinned in the Garden of Eden the body began to die. God had said, "you must not eat from the tree of the knowledge of good and evil, for when you eat of it you will surely die" (Genesis 2:17). When they disobeyed God and ate from the tree, they did die. They died spiritually and were immediately separated from God. They also began to die physically.

As a result of this we know that physical death for us is a part of the process of living; "for "man is destined to die once..." (Hebrews 9:27a). In addition to this termination of human life, another part of this dying process is the many diseases and infirmities that we suffer along the way.

The body that God has given us to dwell in during our earthly years does not belong to us but to someone else. Having placed our faith in Jesus Christ as Savior, our bodies now belong to God. "Do you not know that your body is a temple of the Holy Spirit, who is in you, whom you have received from God? You are not your own; you were bought at a price. Therefore honor God with your body" (1 Corinthians 6:19). Our body is the temple in which the Holy Spirit of God dwells. Consequently, we are to take care of that property which belongs to God.

Not only does your body belong to God, but once you are married your body belongs to your spouse. It is under the authority of your spouse. "The wife's body does not belong to her alone but also to her husband. In the same way the husband's body does not belong to him alone but also to his wife" (1 Corinthians 7:4). While it is true that Paul is speaking specifically about the sexual union in marriage, this principle can be extended to the general concept of caring for one's physical health in marriage.

The physical health of the individual marriage partners has a tremendous effect upon their relationship. They need to be expressing and providing care and concern for the physical welfare of one another. There needs to be complete honesty in this area, as in every other area of the relationship. Personal, physical health is a life-long issue in the marriage, even though it is not often an issue which is discussed during the engagement period. Because it is such an integral part of daily life, it is not something that can be ignored and just allowed to "happen." It must be discussed; beginning in the engagement period.

A number of questions are provided at the end of this chapter to help you begin or continue your discussion in this important area of daily life.

Housing, Education, Employment

Many of the desires and ideas that you have regarding housing, education, and employment are preconceptions based upon your experiences as you grew up in your parents' home. Those desires and ideas were formulated in your mind when you were an individual unit, but <u>now</u> you are part of a couple. Those desires and ideas must now be brought together and discussed within the framework of your relationship with your partner. Then joint decisions, which are mutually agreeable, can be made and steps taken to make them a reality.

Where are you going to live? Will it be in the city, the suburbs, or in a rural area? Will it be in an apartment, a mobile home, a house? Will you pay rent or have a mortgage?

Who is going to be working outside of the home? Will this be full-time employment for both or part-time? Who is going to be the <u>primary</u> supporter of the family?

What about continuing education for one or both of you? Who is going to go to school, and what is the ultimate goal of that education? How are you going to balance the complex time demands upon your relationship while this education is in process?

Many issues need to be discussed in these three specific areas. This discussion is not something that is done one time and then forgotten about. As personal and family circumstances change, these matters will continually come back to the fore-front of attention. Dreams and goals will change, and with them the necessary steps to take in each of these areas will also change. So again, the engagement period is a time to begin to discuss the basic issues of daily living together. For it is here that bond of love is daily hammered out and strengthen in a life-long commitment to one another.

Leisure Time

When we consider the resources that God has given to us, we generally focus our attention upon money or the accumulation of things. One area that we consistently fail to consider, however, is a very important resource: time.

Regardless of who we are, where we are, our financial status, or any other factor, all of us have exactly the same amount of time at our daily disposal. We each have twenty-four hours (3,600 minutes, 86,400 seconds). What are we individually going to do with them? How are we going to invest them?

Previously this was not a problem, for you just did what you wanted to do. But all of that has now changed! There is no longer just one person to consider for you are now a couple, and those twenty-four hours belong to both of you.

Generally, only ten to eleven hours each day are involved in working and its attendant needs. What about the other thirteen to fourteen hours? Naturally some of these will be spent sleeping, but what about the remainder? After you are married, how are you going to spend them?

What about friends with whom you will spend some of these leisure hours? Will they be your friends, your partner's friends, or friends that you both have? There are no "hard and fast" rules when it comes to friendships. Now is the time to begin developing "mutual" friends. Begin to partially step away from "my" friends and "your" friends, and instead begin to develop friends for you as a couple.

There are some advantages to maintaining previous friendships. As you individually continue to have individual friendships, it will give you new things to discuss with your partner. It will also give you time to fulfill a special interest; maybe something in which your partner is not really interested.

There are some disadvantages as well, which can even be considered as dangers. These friendships can be harmful if they are used as a means of escape by one of the partners. They can be divisive, implying that "this is my friend only; not yours."

The best way to approach friendships made before your marriage occurs is to continue those friendships, and help them become mutual friendships. Then concentrate on building friendships with other couples, for it is these that will be the basis for life-long interaction and encouragement.

To help you begin discussing these matters, questions are again provided for your interaction.

QUESTIONS FOR PERSONAL REFLECTION AND COUPLE INTERACTION

Physical Health

1. Do you think a person should be "really" sick before going to a doctor?

2. How do you feel about regular check-ups?

3. When was the last time you went to see a doctor, and what was the reason?

4. Do you have any problems healthwise, such as hypoglycemia, diabetes, frequent headaches, acid stomach, heart problems, cancer, etc.?

5. Do you know of any genetic factors in your make-up that could affect your children? If so, what are they?

6. When you are sick, do you like attention and sympathy, or do you prefer to be left alone?

7. Do you have medical insurance?

Housing, Employment, Education

1. Where are you going to live after the wedding?

2. Are you planning to rent or purchase housing?

3. How are you going to furnish your new home? What style of home decor will you have? Who will decide how to decorate your home?

4. What will be the husband's employment after the wedding?

5. What are his long-range employment goals (5, 10, 15, 20 years from now)?

6. Will the wife work outside of the home? Why or why not?

7. Will you need to be dependent upon her income for meeting financial responsibilities?

8. Are either of you planning to continue your education after the wedding? What are your ultimate educational goals?

9. How much pressure will this put upon your finances? Upon your time together?

10. If your wife becomes pregnant, how will this affect your plans?

Leisure Time-Recreation

1. What do you like to do in your free time?

2. What three activities do you enjoy doing together?

3. What kinds of activities will you want to continue doing separately once you are married?

4. Name two things that your partner enjoys that you could learn to enjoy with him or her.

5. What is your idea of a "great" evening out?

6. What is your idea of a "great" vacation?

7. What friendships do you have that you will continue after the wedding?

8. What mutual friends do you and your partner have?

13

The Wedding Ceremony

Rev. Richard W. Gilbert

For months the planning has occurred, the dozens of last minute details slowly being worked out. Now that special day is fast approaching; the day in which you will commit your love to one another for a lifetime. Marriage is much more than a contract. It is a covenant relationship between the individual partners and God. As that covenant is made, it is a time of celebration with family and friends.

This will be your day; a day in which many memories will be built! It is the day to which you have long looked forward. Over the months you have received hundreds of suggestions from family and friends; some of which you have graciously heard and set aside, others of which you have chosen to implement.

The ceremony that you will soon share is one which you have carefully thought about and planned. It will convey the sanctity of the marriage relationship. It will communicate to your guests that your new life together is centered in God. As much as possible the ceremony will reflect your specific desires and interests. The amount of freedom that you have for the design of the ceremony may vary considerably. Some couples will have minimal input to its format, while others will determine almost every part of it. The minister with whom you are counseling generally has a basic wedding ceremony format that he follows. It is something that he has developed over numerous weddings; finding that this sequence works the best. It is not, however, etched in concrete and is usually open to modification. You will find that he is willing to work with you; to make your ceremony as personal and special for you as he can.

As you look forward to that day, there are many questions to be asked, many problems to be solved, and many plans to be made. Generally, the best rule of thumb for planning the ceremony is "start early!" Don't wait until the last minute. Months are preferable to weeks for the numerous steps of preparation.

To assist you in the planning process, Appendix A contains numerous checklists, forms, and sample information. All are provided to make your wedding ceremony a special celebration and memory.

In addition to the information provided there, the questions that follow are specifically designed to help in your planning process.

QUESTIONS FOR PERSONAL REFLECTION AND COUPLE INTERACTION

1. What kind of mood or atmosphere do you wish to convey at your wedding?

2. What specific ideas do you have to create that atmosphere?

3. How many people do you plan to have in your wedding party (including maid of honor, best man, bridesmaids, groomsmen, and ushers, ring-bearer, flower girl)?

4. What do you plan to do regarding flowers? Photographs? Instrumental music? Vocal music?

5. Will it be a single or double ring ceremony?

6. Will you have a candle ceremony, lighting of a unity candle?

7. What type of wedding vows are you going to say to one another? Traditional? Develop your own?

8. What kind of a reception are you planning? Cake and punch? Light refreshments? Full dinner?

9. Are you planning on entertainment at the reception?

10. Who will be paying for the wedding?

11. In the space below, list all of the expenses for your wedding. Be sure to include everything, so that there are no hidden surprises. Compare these figures with any previously budgeted number. Some of these items will be essential, while others may be optional.

14

Honeymoon Adventure

All of the weeks of planning have come to an end. All of the preparation has been completed. The ceremony and the reception are now history. You have left the church, gone to a prearranged location to change into more comfortable clothing in which to travel. You are <u>now</u> ready to begin your honeymoon. And you are exhausted: physically and emotionally!

Many couples make the mistake of trying to drive too far on the first day, after all of the hustle and bustle of the ceremony and reception. Others have their honeymoon packed so full that there aren't two spare minutes anywhere to just relax and be together. And then there are some who have no plan of any type for their honeymoon.

A successful honeymoon requires very careful planning by <u>both</u> of the marriage partners. This planning cannot be left until the week before the wedding but should be started two to three months in advance.

In the initial planning stage, an essential rule of thumb is "absolute honesty." Don't say that you would like to do one thing when you really mean that you would like to do something else. This honeymoon is for both of you and should be designed by both of you.

Don't pack the honeymoon so full of activities that you have no time just to be with one another. It is not the time to go mountain climbing or whitewater rafting with a group down the Colorado River. There can and should be exciting things to do together, but there should also be adequate time alone. If you are so busy doing things, you will not have time to truly enjoy one another. You need time to walk together in the moonlight, hold one another's hands, time for easy and unhurried conversation, warm embraces and caresses, and loving sexual intimacy.

Try to remember that not everything planned will work out. There are always unexpected "glitches" that will unravel the best plans. When these happen, exercise your sense of humor and make the best of it. These may be unexpected blessings and may even help to make a very special memory.

Determine ahead of time how much money you can afford to

spend on your honeymoon; allocating certain amounts to certain days. Then, without hesitation and with abundant joy, spend it together. It is no longer his money or her money, but it is now our money. You are beginning a lifetime of joint money decisions. These decisions should begin back here in the planning stage for your honeymoon.

Be sure to plan together your wedding night. Don't leave the events to chance but make some definite decisions. How late will you stay up? When it is time to go to bed together, who will undress where? Will the lights be on or off?

Don't place an overemphasis on sexual intercourse. It is God-given and certainly to be enjoyed, but placing the emphasis there will lead to disappointment. Instead, emphasize loving and caring for one another. The physical relationship will be a natural, normal result of this.

You have been building your relationship together over the past months. The honeymoon is the culmination of that building process. It is much more than that, however, for it is the commencement of a lifetime together; a lifetime of commitment, of becoming one!

There are many factors to take into consideration when planning your honeymoon. The questions that follow are designed to assist you in this planning process.

QUESTIONS FOR PERSONAL REFLECTION AND COUPLE INTERACTION

1. Where would you like to go on your honeymoon?

2. How much time do you have available?

3. How much money do you have available to spend?

4. What types of activities do you want to do?

5. What kind of memories do you want to have?

6. What part will sexual intercourse play on your wedding night?

7. What will you feel and do if for some reason you are not able to have sexual intercourse on your wedding night?

8. What expectations do you have of yourself? Of your partner? What fears do you have?

15

Sex In Marriage

The material in this manual has one purpose, and that is to prepare the couple for their marriage. Up until this point the focus has been upon the relationship prior to marriage. In this chapter the setting changes from before the marriage to after the wedding ceremony has taken place. As you read these pages, however, you are still not married. Consequently there are some inherent dangers in the topic of discussion in this chapter.

The writer of Hebrews said, "marriage should be honored by all, and the marriage bed kept pure".[50] The Apostle Paul, in his advice on marriage wrote,

> Since there is so much immorality, each man should have his own wife, and each woman her own husband. The husband should fulfill his marital duty to his wife, and likewise the wife to her husband. The wife's body does not belong to her alone but also to her husband. In the same way, the husband's body does not belong to him alone but also to his wife. Do not deprive each other except by mutual consent and for a time, so that you may devote yourselves to prayer. Then come together again so that Satan will not tempt you because of your lack of self-control.[51]

God designed the sexual relationship to be enjoyed by both men and women only within the marriage relationship.

It is not our purpose in this chapter to discuss specific details of the sexual relationship but instead to set some general guidelines. There are many excellent resources available today to help couples in this area.[52] I want to encourage you to purchase some of these resources and begin reading them _after_ the honeymoon. Please don't begin to read these before you are married, otherwise you will do yourself and your partner a great disservice.

In order to help insure your individual and mutual purity until the wedding night, you need to take many precautions. One of these precautions is the things that your heart and mind feeds upon. The Apostle Paul advises Christians, "whatever is true, whatever is noble, whatever is right, whatever is pure, whatever is lovely, whatever is admirable--if anything is excellent or praiseworthy--think about such things."[53]

There is nothing intrinsically wrong with marriage manuals. They are written to help you in this specific area of marital adjustment, and many are written from a Christian perspective. The danger of studying them before your wedding is the increased interest and emotional excitement that will result. Time spent focusing there before the wedding will push you onto "very thin sexual ice". Wait until your honeymoon, or even after the honeymoon, before you begin to carefully read through these resources. These contain much helpful information, which will only be helpful if it is introduced into your relationship after the wedding.

Some practical suggestions are offered to help you begin your sexual adjustment in marriage. First, keep your sexual relationship with your spouse very private. It is no one else's business what goes on between the two of you in this area. Do not share the topic or any of the intimacies with anyone. This is something that is very private and special between the two of you. Just as you would not physically expose your partner's nakedness to anyone else, don't do it verbally!

Second, be patient with yourself and with your partner. You may or may not bring satisfaction to your partner or experience it yourself. Neither of you is or ever will be an expert in love-making. Sexual intimacy is shared together and learned throughout a lifetime. There will be fantastic times and times that are not fantastic. Throughout all of them you are drawing closer and closer to one another and your relationship becomes increasingly more enjoyable.

Third, discuss your physical relationship with your spouse. Be open and honest about how you feel about certain things your partner does or does not do. Your partner will not know what you like or do not like if you do not communicate openly. Clear and open communication is absolutely crucial in the enjoyment of your sexual relationship. The more that you talk, the more you will learn; and the more you learn, the more mutual enjoyment will result.

Fourth, keep your sexual relationship in proper perspective. A satisfying sexual relationship is the outgrowth of an already satisfying relationship. It is the result, the final brush stroke on the canvas of intimacy painted in every other area of your relationship. Sexual intercourse does not build intimacy in your relationship, but is a very special, very tender, <u>expression of</u> the intimacy that you share with one another.

Finally, discuss together, agree upon, and take joint-responsibility for birth-control measures. Birth control is the responsibility of both partners in the marriage. Which methods are available should be discussed, carefully evaluated, and a specific method or methods chosen. If a chemical means of birth control is chosen, such as a birth control pill, be aware that most of these are abortifacients. An abortifacient does not prevent conception, but it prevents implantation in the uterine walls after conception has taken place. Ask your doctor if the particular pill being prescribed prevents conception.

The sexual relationship is a very special gift from God; to be enjoyed together throughout the life time of your marriage.

<u>QUESTIONS FOR PERSONAL REFLECTION
AND COUPLE INTERACTION</u>

1. How important do you think the sexual relationship is in marriage? How important is it to you? How important do you think it is to your fiancé?

2. What level or amount of sexual experience have you had in the past?

3. What books have you read on the matter of sex in marriage?

4. What form of birth control are you going to practice? Who has made this decision? Who is going to be responsible for its implementation?

16

Family Planning

When God placed mankind upon the earth, in the Garden of Eden, he made both a male and a female. In his infinite wisdom, God had designed the way for the propagation of the species. When He blessed them, God's words to this first couple were "Be fruitful and increase in number; fill the earth and subdue it".[54] When Noah and his family came out of the ark, God's command to them was "Be fruitful and increase in number and fill the earth."[55]

It is fairly obvious that mankind has done a pretty good job of "filling the earth." Current population statistics indicate that the population of the earth is approximately 7.8 billion people (2020). Projected future population varies in estimates, with a low figure showing a world population of 8.9 billion by the year 2035 AD.

The Bible has much to say about families and the interaction between the members of the family. It has much to say about how children are to respond and how they are to be cared for by the parents. In the midst of a world that has gone mad with the destruction of children through abortion and child abuse, it is essential to see the value that God places upon children.

Children are a gift from God[56]; for it is He who determines whether or not a woman will conceive.[57] They are a blessing and a heritage to their parents. "Sons are a heritage from the Lord, children a reward from him. Like arrows in the hands of a warrior are sons born in one's youth. Blessed is the man whose quiver is full of them".[58]

Children enrich a home as no other person or thing can. Children bring life, vitality, freshness and constant daily challenges into the lives of their parents. Children are like seasoning that is put onto a roast that is cooking. The roast is OK by itself, but the flavor lacks something. When the seasonings are added, the flavor is greatly enhanced. That is what children do to a marriage and a home. They enhance the home; making it so much better!

It has been said that the surest way to have a family is not to plan for one. As you love, care for, and share that special intimacy between husband and wife, God may choose to bless your home with children. If He does this, are you ready for the responsibility and the changes that it will bring into your life?

The presence of children in a marriage brings many changes. The privacy that you have as a couple changes, for a third person is now living in your home. The time that you had together must now be shared with this third person; one who demands so much of your time. The energy that you had to do things together is greatly diminished, because so much of it is now spent in meeting the needs of the new family member. The apartment may now be too small; necessitating a move to a two bedroom residence. The extra money is no longer available, because of all the added expense. The freedom to do whatever you want at any time is now changed to activities around the baby's schedule.

At the same time, a whole new world of interests, of goals, dreams has opened up for you. Now the future is no longer just the two of you, but it is a future for three or more. It is a future that now spans the generations; not ending with the end of your lives. It is a future in which you watch and help your children pursue and attain their dreams. It is a future in which you teach your children and grandchildren of personal faith in Jesus Christ.

During this engagement period you need to discuss this vital topic. Do you want to have children? How many would you like to have? How soon do you wish to begin your family? How would you respond to an unexpected pregnancy? If you were unable to have children, would you consider adoption? These are all questions that need to be discussed now, before the wedding. This is a decision that you must make and follow together.

QUESTIONS FOR PERSONAL REFLECTION
AND COUPLE INTERACTION

1. Do you want to have children? How many?

2. Why do you wish to have children?

3. Do you think that the presence of children will make changes in your home? In what ways?

4. If you do not wish to have children, why not?

5. How soon do you wish to start a family?

6. How would you handle an unexpected pregnancy?

7. If you are unable to have children, would you consider adoption? Would you adopt only a baby or an older child?

Appendix A

BRIDE'S PERSONAL INFORMATION

Name _____

Address _____

Telephone No._____

Date of Birth _____   Age _____

Parent's Name _____

Parent's Address _____

Your parents' response to your contemplated marriage?

Father_____   Mother_____

Your previous marital status:

Never Married _____Divorced _____

Widower _____Annulled _____

How long have you been a Christian? _____

Of what church are you a member? _____

_____

Are you now pregnant? _____

If you become pregnant before the wedding, you MUST notify this pastor!

GROOM'S

PERSONAL INFORMATION

Name _____

Address _____

Telephone No. _____

Date of Birth_____ Age_____

Parent's Name _____

Parent's Address _____

Your parents' response to you contemplated marriage?

Father_____ Mother_____

Your previous marital status:

Never married _____ Divorced _____

Widower_____ Annulled _____

How long have you been a Christian? _____

Of what church are you a member?_____

GENERAL WEDDING

PLANNING FORM

Rehearsal Date _____   Time _____

    Location _____

Ceremony Date _____   Time_____

    Location _____

Reception Date _____   Time _____

    Location _____

Maid (Matron of Honor) _____

Bridesmaids _____

_____

_____

_____

Flower Girl _____

Best Man _____

Groomsmen _____

_____

_____

Ring Bearer _____

Ushers

_____

_____

_____

Organist _____

Pianist _____

Special Music _____

Florist _____

Cake _____

Photographer _____

Video _____

Sound System _____

Custodian _____

Officiant _____

Anticipated number of guests:

    Ceremony _____   Reception _____

SAMPLE WEDDING CEREMONY

Organ Prelude
Lighting of Individual Candles
Seating of Mothers
Special Music Presentation
Processional
Welcome and Scriptural Basis for Marriage
Invocation
Parents' Approval and Affirmation
Giving Away of Bride
Personal Glimpse of Bride and Groom
Wedding Message
Special Music Presentation
Personal Charge to Couple
Wedding Vows
Ring Ceremony
Prayer of Dedication
Pronouncement of Marriage
Wedding Kiss
Unity Candle Ceremony
Presentation of Couple
Recessional

SAMPLE WEDDING VOWS-I

To the Husband:

___(Name)___, will you have this woman to be your wedded wife, to live together after God's holy estate of marriage? Will you love, respect, comfort, honor, and serve her? Will you always be honest with her and stand by her side whatever may come? Will you keep her in sickness and in health, and forsaking all others keep yourself only unto her, so long as you both shall live? If so, say "I will."

To the Wife:

___(Name)___, will you have this man to be your wedded husband, to live together after God's holy estate of marriage? Will you love, respect, comfort, honor, and serve him? Will you always be honest with him and stand by his side whatever may come? Will you keep him in sickness and in health, and forsaking all others keep yourself only unto him, so long as you both shall live? If so, say "I will."

SAMPLE WEDDING VOWS-II

Husband:

"I, __(Name)__, take you __(Name)__, to be my wedded wife; to have and to hold from this day forward; for better for worse, for richer for poorer, in sickness, and in health, to love and to cherish, until at death we part. According to God's holy ordinance, I give you this pledge."

Wife:

"I, __(Name)__, take you __(Name)__, to be my wedded husband; to have and to hold from this day forward; for better for worse, for richer for poorer, in sickness and in health, to love and to cherish, until at death we part. According to God's holy ordinance, I give you this pledge."

SAMPLE WEDDING HYMNS

A Wedding Benediction (solo)
A Wedding Prayer (solo)
Children of the Heavenly Father
Each for the Other (solo)
For the Beauty of the Earth
From God I Ne'er Will Turn Me (Buxtehude)
God of Our Fathers
Great Is Thy Faithfulness
Holy, Holy, Holy
How Firm a Foundation
Jesus, Joy of Man's Desiring (Bach)-Organ
Jesus, the Very Thought of Thee
Love Divine, All Love Excelling
May Jesus Christ Be Praised
My Jesus, I Love Thee
O Could I Speak the Matchless Worth
O Happy Home
O Jesus I Have Promised
O Master, Let Me Walk with Thee
O Perfect Love (solo)
O Promise Me (solo)
Prelude and Fugue in C Major (Bach)-Organ
Rejoice Greatly, O My Soul (Karg-Elert)
Rejoice, Ye Pure in Heart
Reverie (Debussy)-Organ
Savior, Like a Shepherd Lead Us
Serenade (Shubert)-Organ
Suite Gothique (Boellmann)
The King of Love My Shepherd
Thou Glorious Bridegroom (Wedding Prayer)
Trumpet Voluntary (Purcell)-Trumpet or Organ
We Give Thee But Thine Own

CONTEMPORARY

RELIGIOUS WEDDING MUSIC

All of Me-Michael Sweet
Bridal Prayer-Roger Copeland
Cherish the Treasure-John Mohr
He Has Chosen You for Me-Pat Terry
Household of Faith-John Rosasco
I've Waited a Lifetime-Tim Sheppard
I Will Be Here-Steven Curtis Chapman
Love of My Life-Sheila Walsh and Chris Eaton
Make Us One-Denise and Dwight Liles
My Treasure-Scott Wesley Brown
One Hand, One Heart-Stephen Sondheim and Leonard Bernstein
Only God Could Love You More-Dwight Liles and Niles Borup
Parent's Prayer-Greg Davis
The Father Says, 'I Do'-Brent Lamb
The Gift of Love-Hal Hapon (arr.)
This is the Day-Scott Wesley Brown
Wedding Prayer-Fern Glasgow Dunlap
Wedding Prayer-Mary Rice
Wedding Song-Paul Stookey
We've Only Just Begun-Roger Nichols and Paul Williams
With This Ring-Remus Harris and John Sacco

SECULAR

WEDDING MUSIC

Always-Jonathan Lewis, David Lewis, Wayne Lewis
Always and Forever-Rod Temperton
Close to You-Burt Bacharach
Endless Love-Lionel Richie
Everything I Do, I Do It for You-Bryan Adams, Robert John Lange, Michael Kumen
Follow Me-John Denver
I Will Always Love You-Dolly Parton
Longer-Daniel Fogelberg
Lost in Your Eyes-Debby Gibson
The Greatest Love of All-Michael Masser
Theme from Ice Castles-Marvin Hamlisch
To Me-Mack David, Mike Reid
Truly-Lionel Richie
You and I-Frank Myers
You Are So Beautiful-Billy Preston and Bruce Fisher
You're the Inspiration-Peter Cetera and David Foster

BRIDE'S WEDDING CHECKLIST

Six to Three Months

1. Discuss available finances
2. Decide style of wedding
3. Begin pre-marital counseling with minister who will perform the service
4. Set date on church calendar
5. Contact instrumentalists and soloists
6. Plan the reception
   a. Reserve location
   b. Catering, music, etc.
7. Select wedding attendants
8. Select wedding gown and attendants' gowns
9. Order invitations and announcements
10. Reserve photographer
11. Begin planning honeymoon

Two Months

1. Order flowers
2. Register at stores for wedding gifts
3. Select attendants' gifts and bridegroom's gift
4. Purchase groom's ring
5. Order wedding cake

One Month

1. Mail invitations
2. Get marriage license with fiancé
3. Plan music with fiancé and organist

Two Weeks

1. Check on wedding gowns
2. Determine reception seating arrangements
3. Begin moving personal items to new residence

One Week

1. Check on florist, photographer, caterer, organist, soloist
2. Prepare clothing for wedding day
3. Attend rehearsal and rehearsal dinner; give gifts to attendants
4. Flowers, bows, etc. at church
5. Rest

Wedding Day

1. Enjoy the day
2. Give gift to groom

GROOM'S WEDDING CHECKLIST

Six to Three Months

1. Make guest list
2. Purchase bride's wedding ring
3. Begin pre-marital counseling
4. Select attendants
5. Plan honeymoon with fiancé
6. Order tuxedos for self and attendants

Two Months

1. Reserve location for rehearsal dinner

One Month

1. Purchase gifts for attendants and bride
2. Get marriage license with fiancé
3. Complete any final honeymoon plans

One Week

1. Move personal items to future residence
2. Prepare clothing for wedding day
3. Attend rehearsal and rehearsal dinner; give gifts to attendants
4. Rest

Wedding Day

1. Enjoy the day
2. Give gift to bride

DUTIES OF THE WEDDING PARTY

Best Man

1. Emotional support for groom
2. Attendance at rehearsal
3. Signature as witness to the wedding
4. Delivery of "love-gifts" to the organist, soloist, etc.
5. May hold the bride's wedding ring until the appropriate time in the ceremony
6. Stand in receiving line with rest of wedding party
7. May act as moderator at the wedding reception
8. Leads in "toast" to the newlyweds

Maid (Matron) of Honor

1. Emotional support for bride
2. Attendance at rehearsal
3. Signature as witness to the wedding
4. Helps bride dress for the ceremony
5. Holds bride's bouquet during the service
6. May hold the groom's wedding ring until the appropriate time in the ceremony.
7. Arranges bride's train as needed during the ceremony
8. Stand in receiving line with rest of wedding party

Bridesmaids and Groomsmen

1. Emotional support for the bride and groom
2. Attendance at rehearsal and rehearsal dinner
3. Participation in the ceremony with the bride and groom
4. Stand in receiving line with rest of wedding party

Ushers

1. Primary duty is to see that all guests are properly escorted and seated; facing the platform, left is the bride's side and right the groom's side
2. Dismissal of guests at end of ceremony

Appendix B

MONTHLY BUDGET FOR FIRST YEAR

FIXED EXPENSES

Housing:

Rent	$_____
Mortgage Payments	$_____
Taxes, assessments	$_____

Utilities:

Gas	$_____
Electric	$_____
Phone	$_____
Water	$_____
Sewer	$_____

Insurance Premiums:

Auto	$_____
Life	$_____
Health	$_____
Homeowners, Tenets	$_____

Debt Retirement:

Loans	$_____
Credit Card	$_____
Contributions to Church	$_____

Professional or Union Dues $_____
Organizational Membership $_____
Vehicle Licenses $_____
Regular Savings $_____

FLEXIBLE EXPENSES

Living Expenses:
    Food and Household Supplies $_____
    Laundry and Cleaning $_____
    Personal Care Items $_____
    Newspaper, Magazines, etc. $_____
Personal Allowance $_____
Transportation:
    Auto Operation $_____
    Auto Maintenance $_____
Clothing $_____
Medical and Dental Care $_____
Education $_____
Entertainment, recreation, etc. $_____
Furniture, household repairs $_____
Gifts $_____
TOTAL MONTHLY EXPENSES $_____

Total Monthly Income (All Sources) $_____
    (minus) -
Total Monthly Expenses $_____
    (equals) =

**TOTAL MONTHLY
CASH RESERVE** $_____

Appendix C

SUGGESTED PRE-MARITAL
COUNSELING SCHEDULE

Session 1

Administer Prepare/Enrich
Assessment test
Get to know the couple

Session 2

Prepare/Enrich follow-up

Session 3

Prepare/Enrich follow-up

Session 4

Pre-Marital Counseling Manual, chapters 1-2

Session 5

PMC Manual, chapters 3-4

Session 6

PMC Manual, chapters 5-6

Session 7

PMC Manual, chapter 7

Session 8

PMC Manual, chapters 8-9

Session 9

PMC Manual, chapter 10

Session 10

PMC Manual, chapters 11-12

Session 11

PMC Manual, chapter 13

Session 12

PMC Manual, chapters 14-16

Bibliography of Resources Cited

Arndt, William F. and F. Wilbur Gingrich. <u>A Greek-English Lexicon of the New Testament and Other Early Christian Literature</u> (BAGD), 1979 ed.

Benson, Dan. <u>The Total Man</u>. Wheaton, IL: Tyndale House Publishers, Inc., 1982.

Browning, Elizabeth Barrett. <u>Sonnets from the Portugese</u>, Sonnet XIV. Kansas City, MO: Hallmark Card, Inc.

Burkett, Larry. <u>Your Finances in Changing Times</u>. Chicago: Moody Press, 1975.

Clinebell, Howard and Charlotte Clinebell. <u>The Intimate Marriage</u>. New York: Harper & Row Publishers, Inc., 1970.

Elliott, Elisabeth. <u>Passion and Purity</u>. Old Tappan, NJ: Fleming H. Revell Company, 1984.

Fryling, Robert and Alice Fryling. <u>A Handbook for Engaged Couples</u>. Downers Grove, IL: InterVarsity Press, 1977.

Getz, Gene. <u>A Biblical Theology of Material Possessions</u>. Chicago: Moody Press, 1990.

LaHaye, Tim and Beverly LaHaye. The Act of Marriage. Grand Rapids: Zondervan, 1976.

Landis, Judson T. and Mary G. Landis. Personal Adjustment, Marriage and Family Living. Englewood Cliffs, NJ: Prectice-Hall, Inc., 1966.

Miles, Herbert J. Sexual Happiness in Marriage. Grand Rapids: Zondervan Publishing House, 1967.

Penner, Clifford and Joyce Penner. The Gift of Sex. Waco: Word, Inc., 1981.

Powell, John. Why Am I Afraid to Tell You Who I Am? Niles, IL: Argus Communications, 1969.

The Holy Bible: New International Version. International Bible Society, 1973.

Webster's Seventh New Collegiate Dictionary. 1963 ed.

Wheat, Ed and Gaye Wheat. Love Life for Every Married Couple. Grand Rapids: Zondervan Publishing House, 1980.

Wright, H. Norman. Communications: Key to Your Marriage. Ventura, CA: Regal Books, 1985.

Bibliography for Marriage Enrichment

General Marriage Resources

Arp, Dave and Claudia Arp. 60 One-Minute Marriage Builders. Brentwood, TN: Wolgemuth and Hyatt, 1989.

Benson, Dan. The Total Man. Wheaton, IL: Tyndale House Publishers, Inc., 1982.

Christenson, Larry. The Christian Family. Minneapolis, Minn.: Bethany Fellowship, 1970.

Klever, Phil. Are We Having Fun Yet?: Working Together to Create a Loving Marriage. St. Paul, MN: International Marriage Encounter, 1988.

LaHaye, Tim. How to Be Happy Though Married. Wheaton: Tyndale House Publishers, 1981.

Landis, Judson T. and Mary G. Landis. Personal Adjustment, Marriage and Family Living. Englewood Cliffs, NJ: Prectice-Hall, Inc., 1966.

Schaeffer, Edith. What Is a Family? Old Tappan, NJ: Fleming H. Revell, 1975.

Wheat, Ed and Gaye Wheat. Love Life for Every Married Couple. Grand Rapids: Zondervan Publishing House, 1980.

Communications

MacDonald, Gail and Gordon MacDonald. If Those Who Reach Could Touch. Old Tappan, NJ: Fleming H. Revell Co., 1984.

Miller, Sherod, Phillis Miller, Elam Nunnally, and Daniel Wackman. Talking and Listening Together. St. Paul, MN: International Marriage Encounter, 1988.

Wright, H. Norman. Communications: Key to Your Marriage. Ventura, A: Regal Books, 1985.

Wright, H. Norman. How to Speak your Spouse's Language. Old Tappan, NJ: Fleming H. Revell, 1986.

Conflict Resolution

Dobson, James. What Wives Wish Their Husbands Knew about Women. Wheaton, Ill.: Tyndale, 1975.

Wright, H. Norman. Communications: Key to Your Marriage. Ventura, CA: Regal Books, 1985.

Wright, H. Norman. The Pillars of Marriage. Glendale, CA: Regal Books, 1980.

Shedd, Charlie. Letters to Karen. New York: Avon Books, 1965.

Shedd, Charlie. Letters to Philip. New York: Pyramid Books, 1969.

Emotional Adjustments

Lutzer, Erwin. Managing Your Emotions. Wheaton, IL: Victor Books, 1984.

Mace, David. Love and Anger. Grand Rapids: Zondervan Books, 1982.

Oliver, Gary and H. Norman Wright. When Anger Hits Home. Chicago: Moody Press, 1992.

Powell, John. Fully Human Fully Alive. Niles, IL: Argus Communications, 1976.

Family Adjustments

Wright, H. Norman. In-Laws, Outlaws. Irvine, CA: Harvest House Publishers, 1977.

Financial Management

Burkett, Larry. Your Finances in Changing Times. Chicago: Moody Press, 1975.

Burkett, Larry. Debt-Free Living. Chicago: Moody Press, 1989.

Burkett, Larry. The Complete Financial Guide for Young Couples. Wheaton, IL: Victor Books, 1989.

Fooshee, George Jr. You Can Be Financially Free. Old Tappan, NJ: Fleming H. Revell, 1976.

Getz, Gene. A Biblical Theology of Material Possessions. Chicago: Moody Press, 1990.

Romance

Bundschuh, Rick and Dave Gilbert. Romance Rekindled. Eugene, OR: Harvest House Publishers, 1988.

Wright, H. Norman. Holding On to Romance. Ventura, CA: Regal Books, 1992.

Sexual Adjustment

Clinebell, Howard and Charlotte Clinebell. The Intimate Marriage. New York: Harper & Row Publishers, Inc., 1970.

Heiman, Julia and Joseph LoPiccolo. Becoming Orgasmic. New York: Prentice Hall, 1988.

Hendrix, Harville. Getting the Love You Want: A Guide for Couples. New York: Harper and Row, 1990.

LaHaye, Tim and Beverly LaHaye. The Act of Marriage. Grand Rapids: Zondervan, 1976.

Miles, Herbert J. Sexual Happiness in Marriage. Grand Rapids: Zondervan Publishing House, 1982.

Penner, Clifford and Joyce Penner. The Gift of Sex: A Couple's Guide to Sexual Fulfillment. Waco: Word, Inc., 1981.

Penner, Clifford and Joyce Penner. Sex Facts for the Family. Dallas: Word, Inc., 1992.

Penner, Clifford and Joyce Penner. 52 Ways to Have Fun, Fantastic Sex. Nashville: Thomas Nelson Publishers, 1994.

Wheat, Ed and Gaye Wheat. <u>Intended for Pleasure</u>. Old Tappan, NJ: Fleming H. Revell, 1979.

Wheat, Ed and Gaye Wheat. <u>Sex Technique and Sex Problems in Marriage</u> (Audio Cassette). Springdale, AR: Bible Believers Cassettes, Inc., n.d.

Understanding Partner's Needs

Harley, Willard F., J. <u>His Needs, Her Needs</u>. Old Tappan, NJ: Fleming H. Revell Company, 1986.

Rainey, Dennis and Barbara Rainey. <u>Building Your Mate's Self-Esteem</u>. Nashville: Thomas Nelson Publishers, 1993.

Swihart, Philip. <u>How to Live with Your Feelings</u>. Downers Grove, IL: InterVarsity Press, 1976.

Endnotes

Introduction

1   Prepare/Enrich was developed by David H. Olson, Ph.D. Information can be received about this assessment tool by contacting Prepare/Enrich, Inc., P. O. Box 190, Minneapolis, MN 55458-0190.

Chapter 1

2   Wright, H. Norman. Communications: Key to Your Marriage. Ventura, CA: Regal Books, 1985, p. 12.

Chapter 2

3   Ephesians 5:22-33
4   Ephesians 5:1-21

Chapter 4

5   Clinebell, Howard and Charlotte Clinebell. The Intimate Marriage. New York: Harper & Row Publishers, Inc., 1970, p. 10.
6   Clinebell and Clinebell, p. 58.
7   2 Corinthians 6:14

Chapter 5

8   The Niagara Gazette, October 30, 1993 issue cited an article from the U. S. Center for Disease Control and Prevention. The article stated that since the AIDS epidemic began in 1981 it has struck 339,250 Americans and killed 204,390 of them. It is now the leading cause of death for men aged 25 to 44 years.

9   Marriage was instituted before sin came into the world. God's evaluation of all of his creation was that it was very good (Genesis 1:31).

10   1 Peter 5:8

11   Romans 14:21 "It is better not to eat meat or drink wine or to do anything else that will cause your brother to fall."

12   Adapted from the Lutheran Youth Alive Newsletter.

13   Galatians 5:22-23 "But the fruit of the Spirit is love, joy, peace, patience, kindness, goodness, faithfulness, gentleness, and self-control..."

14   Philippians 4:8 "Finally, brothers, whatever is true, whatever is noble, whatever is right, whatever is pure, whatever is lovely, whatever is admirable—if anything is excellent or praiseworthy--think about such things."

15   Elliott, Elisabeth. Passion and Purity. Old Tappan, NJ: Fleming H. Revell Company, 1984, p. 140.

Chapter 6

16   John 13:34.

17   Dr. Karl Menninger, of the Menninger Clinic.

18   Webster's Third New Collegiate Dictionary, s.v. "love".

19   Arndt, William F. and F. Wilbur Gingrich. A Greek-English Lexicon of the New Testament and Other Early Christian Literature (BAGD), 1979 eds., s.v. "epithumia," p. 293.

20   BAGD, s.v. "phileo," p. 859.

21   BAGD, s.v. "agape," p. 5.

22   Wheat, Ed and Gaye Wheat. Love Life for Every Married Couple. Grand Rapids: Zondervan Publishing House, 1980, pp. 57-129. In chapter 5 Dr. Wheat suggests five different types of love, and then further describes each type in the following five chapters.

23   Proverbs 11:2a; 13:10a; 16:18; 29:32a.

24   Webster's Dictionary, s.v. "rude".

25 BAGD, s.v. "logidzomai," pp. 475-476.

26 BAGD, s.v. "stego," p. 765.

27 Webster's Dictionary, s.v. "hope".

28 Webster's Dictionary, s.v. "perseverance".

29 Browning, Elizabeth Barrett. Sonnets from the Portuguese, Sonnet XIV. Kansas City, MO: Hallmark Card, Inc., 1970.

Chapter 7

30 Webster's Dictionary, s.v. "communication".

31 Clinebell and Clinebell, p. 89.

32 Powell, John. Why Am I Afraid to Tell You Who I AM? Argus Communications, 1969, pp. 91-92.

Chapter 8

33 Webster's Dictionary, s.v. "emotion".

34 Genesis 1:26a.

35 Genesis 1:31.

36 Webster's Dictionary, s.v. "anger".

37 Numbers 32:10-13 refers to the Lord's judgment upon Israel when the spies recommended not going into the land of Canaan. "The Lord's anger was aroused that day and he swore this oath: 'Because they have not followed me wholeheartedly, not one of the men twenty years old or more who came up out of Egypt will see the land I promised on oath to Abraham, Isaac and Jacob - not one except Caleb son of Jephunneh and Kenizzite and Joshua son of Nun, for they followed the Lord wholeheartedly.' The Lord's anger burned against Israel and he made them wander in the desert forty years, until the whole generation of those who had done evil in his sight was gone."

Chapter 9

38 Wright. Communications, pp.139-157; Benson, Dan. The Total Man. Wheaton, Illinois: Tyndale House Publishers, Inc., 1982, pp.170-172;

Fryling, Robert and Alice Fryling. A Handbook for Engaged Couples. Downers Grove, Illinois: InterVarsity Press, 1977, p.22.

39 Ephesians 6:18; Philippians 4:6-7; 1 Thessalonians 5:17; James 4:2-3; 1 Peter 5:7.

Chapter 10

40 1 Timothy 6:10a.
41 1 Timothy 6:10b.
42 1 Corinthians 4:7; Luke 12:15-34.
43 1 Timothy 6:17.
44 Dr. Gene Getz has written an excellent book on the biblical teaching regarding material possessions. Getz, Gene. A Biblical Theology of Material Possessions. Chicago: Moody Press, 1990.
45 Deuteronomy 15:4-6.
46 2 Corinthians 9:7.
47 Luke 16:10-13.
48 Burkett, Larry. Your Finances in Changing Times. Chicago: Moody Press, 1975, pp.152-162.

Chapter 11

49 Landis, Judson T. and Mary G. Landis. Personal Adjustment, Marriage and Family Living. Englewood Cliffs, N.J.: Prentice-Hall, Inc., 1966, pp.238-239.

Chapter 15

50 Hebrews 13:4
51 1 Corinthians 7:2-5.
52 LaHaye, Tim and Beverly LaHaye. The Act of Marriage. Grand Rapids: Zondervan, 1976; Penner, Clifford and Joyce Penner. The Gift of Sex. Waco: Word, Inc., 1981; Wheat, Ed and Gaye Wheat. Intended for Pleasure; Miles, Herbert J. Sexual Happiness in Marriage. Grand Rapids: Zondervan Publishing House, 1967.
53 Philippians 4:8.

Chapter 16

54 Genesis 1:28a.
55 Genesis 9:1.
56 Genesis 33:5.
57 Genesis 20:18; 29:31; Luke 1:31.
58 Psalm 127:3-5a.

Printed in the United States
by Baker & Taylor Publisher Services